Schizophrenia: A Very Short Introduction

Very Short Introductions available now:

For more information visit our web site:
www.oup.co.uk/general/vsi/

Christopher Frith and Eve Johnstone

SCHIZOPHRENIA

A Very Short Introduction

OXFORD
UNIVERSITY PRESS

OXFORD
UNIVERSITY PRESS

Great Clarendon Street, Oxford OX2 6DP

Oxford University Press is a department of the University of Oxford.
It furthers the University's objective of excellence in research, scholarship,
and education by publishing worldwide in

Oxford New York

Auckland Bangkok Buenos Aires Cape Town Chennai
Dar es Salaam Delhi Hong Kong Istanbul Karachi Kolkata
Kuala Lumpur Madrid Melbourne Mexico City Mumbai Nairobi
São Paulo Shanghai Taipei Tokyo Toronto

Oxford is a registered trade mark of Oxford University Press
in the UK and in certain other countries

Published in the United States
by Oxford University Press Inc., New York

British Library Cataloguing in Publication Data

Data available

Library of Congress Cataloging in Publication Data

Data available

ISBN 978-0-19-280221-7

13 15 17 19 20 18 16 14 12

Typeset by RefineCatch Ltd, Bungay, Suffolk
Printed in Great Britain by
Ashford Colour Press Ltd, Gosport, Hampshire

Contents

List of illustrations

The publisher and the authors apologize for any errors or omissions in the above list. If contacted they will be pleased to rectify these at the earliest opportunity.

Chapter 1
The experience of schizophrenia

Schizophrenia is the term applied to a severe form of mental disorder that exists in all countries and cultures and is more prevalent than you might think. At a rough estimate, about 1 person in 100 may experience this disorder at some time in their lives. This lifetime risk of 1% is about the same as that for developing rheumatoid arthritis; many of us will know of someone with this much more visible disorder. Not only is the emotional experience of schizophrenia extremely distressing both for the sufferer and for his or her family and friends, the monetary cost of schizophrenia is also severe. In terms of care and treatment, the annual cost of schizophrenia in the UK in the early 1990s was £397 million, while the indirect costs in terms of lost production were conservatively estimated for the same period as £1.7 billion.

Since most of us have no direct experience of mental disorders, our knowledge of schizophrenia often comes from the popular press. Articles about mental illness are quite frequent, but sufferers and their carers are nearly always portrayed in a negative light. The tabloid papers in particular concentrate on individual cases involving violent death. These can be suicides in striking circumstances, such as the man who entered the lions' den at London Zoo and was severely mauled, or unmotivated murders like the case of Christopher Clunis who stabbed to death a total stranger on the platform of Finsbury Park underground station. From such reports we gain the impression that schizophrenia is a dangerous form of madness. Sufferers from this disorder are irrational and behave in ways that are impossible to understand. In fact, as we shall see, the vast majority of sufferers are not dangerous, and if we are to help them we must try to understand them.

Having said that, it will always be difficult for those of us who are mentally well to understand what it is like to experience schizophrenia. Perhaps the nearest we can get to the experience is by reading what sufferers themselves have said. A particularly memorable account, quoted by Sir Aubrey Lewis in 1967, was written by a boy of 18 years who had been ill for at least a year.

> I am more and more losing contact with my environment and with myself. Instead of taking an interest in what goes on and caring about what happens with my illness, I am all the time losing my emotional contact with everything including myself. What remains is only an abstract knowledge of what goes on around me and of the internal happenings in myself. . . . Even this illness which pierces to the centre of my whole life I can regard only objectively. But, on rare occasions, I am overwhelmed with the sudden realisation of the ghastly destruction that is caused by this creeping uncanny disease that I have fallen a victim to. . . . My despair sometimes floods over me. But after each such outburst I become more indifferent, I lose myself more in the disease, I sink into an almost oblivious existence. My fate when I reflect upon it is the most horrible one can conceive of. I cannot picture anything more frightful than for a well-endowed cultivated human being to live through his own gradual deterioration fully aware of it all the time. But that is what is happening to me.

This account is especially striking because it concerns the so-called 'negative' aspect of schizophrenia – the gradual withdrawal from the world and from the self. Few patients are able to describe their experience in this way; it is precisely because of this loss of contact that the vast majority of sufferers no longer have the ability or the motivation to talk about their illness in such a vivid and compelling fashion. Far more common are accounts of the 'positive' aspect of schizophrenia – the florid false perceptions (hallucinations) and false beliefs (delusions) that are so characteristic of this disorder. Typically these accounts are not written during the period of illness, but after recovery.

This aspect of the illness is illustrated in two famous historical accounts, one from the end of the 17th century and the other from the mid-19th century. We do not have enough information to be certain that George Trosse and John Perceval would have been considered to be suffering from schizophrenia by current diagnostic standards. However, many of their descriptions of their experiences are strikingly similar to accounts given by patients today. Both men clearly describe hallucinations and delusions. These historical accounts also give us an idea of how sufferers were treated in the past.

The Reverend Mr George Trosse, *c.*1690

I was haunted with a great many terrifying and disquieting *Visions and Voices*; which tho' (I believe) they had *no Reality* in themselves, yet they *seem'd* to be *such* to me, and had the *same Effect* upon me, as if they had *been really* what they *appear'd* to be.

I heard a Voice, as I fancy'd, as it were just behind me, saying, *Yet more humble; Yet more humble*; with some continuance.... In Compliance with it I proceeded to pluck down my *Stockings*, and then my *Hose*, and my *Doublet*; and as I was thus uncloathing my self, I had a strong internal Impression, that all was well done, and a full Compliance with the design of the *Voice*.

At length, standing up before the *Window*, I either *heard a Voice*, which bid me, or *had a strong Impulse*, which excited me, to *cut off my Hair*; to which I reply'd, *I have no Scissors.* It was then hinted, that a *Knife would do it*; but I answer'd, *I have none.* Had I had one, I verily believe, this *Voice* would have gone from my *Hair* to my *Throat*, and commanded me to cut it.

These passages come from the life of the Reverend Mr George Trosse, written by himself and published in 1714 shortly after his death. The experiences he describes occurred many years earlier when he was in his early twenties. By the time he came to write about these experiences he was a Presbyterian minister and a respected member of the community in Exeter. At the time of the experiences he was considered to be mad. Since he refused to speak or to eat, or to leave his bed, it is not surprising that his friends became concerned.

I was perswaded that if I was removed out of (my bed), I should fall into *Hell*, and be plung'd into the *Depth of Misery.*

He had to be taken away by force.

They procur'd a *very stout strong Man* to ride before me, and when *he* was on Horseback, they by Force put me up behind *him*, bound me by a strong Linnen-Cloth to *him*; and, because I struggled, and did all I could to throw my self off the Horse, they tied my Legs under the Belly of it.

At last, by God's good Providence, we were brought safely to the *Physicians* house. Here I was committed to a Person who became my *Guardian*, to watch me, that I might not *destroy my self.* And in this Room and House I continu'd several Weeks, nay, as I take it, Months. Sometimes they put Bolts upon my Hands and Fetters on my Feet, when I prov'd *violent* and *unruly* (which I often did); for I would often *strive* and *fight.*

John Perceval, 1838

Over 100 years later, in 1838, John Perceval wrote a lengthy account of his experience of madness. John Perceval was one of 12 children of Spencer Perceval, the only English prime minister to have been assassinated. When John was 27 years old he started seeing visions and hearing voices that told him to do strange things. His behaviour became so erratic that a 'lunatic doctor' was called who strapped him to his bed and gave him broth and medicine. A few days later, John's brother arrived and took him to a private asylum near Bristol which was run by a Dr Fox.

John was kept in asylums for about three years, but he gradually recovered and began writing about his illness a year or so later. He

1. A madhouse scene. Etching by Grant from *Sketches in London* (1838), showing the interior of an unnamed lunatic asylum in London. Inmates draw on the walls, look up at the high windows, or read distractedly.

devoted the rest of his life to trying to reform the way in which the mad were treated.

> Only a short time before I was confined to my bed I began to hear voices, at first only close to my ear, afterwards in my head, or as if one was whispering in my ear, – or in various parts of the room. These voices I obeyed or endeavoured to obey, and believed almost implicitly. . . . Those voices commanded me to do, and made me believe a number of false and terrible things.

> Whilst eating my breakfast, different spirits assailed me, trying me. One said, eat a piece of bread for my sake, &c., &c.; another at the same time would say refuse it for my sake, or, refuse *that piece* for my sake and take *that*; others, in like manner, would direct me to take or refuse my tea. I could seldom refuse one, without disobeying the other. . . . Zachary Gibbs [his attendant] stood by my bed-side observing me in a new character. I understood that he was no longer Zachary Gibbs, but a spiritual body called HERMINET HERBERT. He had put on a nankeen jacket, in order to remind me of the dream, in which the Holy Ghost, who was his mother, had appeared to me, promising never to desert me. That he knew all my thoughts, and all I was inspired to do, and could not be deceived.

As with George Trosse, one of the main features of John Perceval's experience was that voices were continually commanding him to perform various actions. These actions ranged from the trivial to commands to attack people.

> I recollect that even at the height of my delusions I refused to obey these voices on several occasions, when by obeying them I was afraid of taking away the life of my attendants – for instance I was often desired to push a man named Hobbs backwards into an empty bath, but I was afraid to do it, lest I should injure him.

Although there are few first-person accounts of the experience of schizophrenia, there are many accounts of what patients have told their doctors. In order to help a sufferer from mental illness, a doctor will try to find out as much as possible about the patient's experiences and will record what the patient says in more or less detail in the case notes. Accounts of these cases are sometimes published.

The first such accounts to which the term schizophrenia can be applied with any real degree of confidence were by physicians Philippe Pinel and John Haslam, both writing, independently, in 1809. Haslam did describe individual cases, but rather provided a composite account of a form of insanity 'which occurs in young persons'. He was particularly impressed by the negative aspects of schizophrenia. Referring to the onset of this form of the illness, he wrote:

> ... it is almost imperceptible; some months usually elapse before it becomes the subject of particular notice and fond relatives are frequently deceived by the hope that it is only an abatement of excessive vivacity conducing to a prudent reserve and steadiness of character, a degree of apparent thoughtfulness and inactivity precede, together with a diminution of the ordinary curiosity, concerning that which is passing before them; and they, therefore, neglect those objects and pursuits which formerly proved sources of delight and instruction. The sensibility appears considerably blunted; they do not bear the same affection towards their parents and relatives; they become unfeeling to kindness, and careless of reproof ... As their apathy increases, they are negligent of their dress and inattentive to personal cleanliness. Frequently they seem to experience transient impulses of passion, but these have no source in sentiment, the tears which trickle down at one time are as unmeaning as the loud laugh which succeeds them.

In 1860, the French psychologist Benedict Augustin Morel introduced the term 'démence précoce' to describe an adolescent patient, once bright and active, who had slowly lapsed into a state of withdrawal.

Gradually he lost his cheerfulness, became gloomy, taciturn and showed a tendency towards solitude.... The young patient progressively forgot everything he had learned. His so brilliant intellectual faculties underwent in time a very distressing arrest. A kind of torpor akin to hebetude replaced the earlier activity and when I saw him, I concluded that the fatal transition to the state of démence précoce was about to take place.... A sudden paralysis of the faculties in démence précoce indicates that the patient has reached the end of his intellectual life that he can control.

Haslam and Morel gave detailed accounts of individual cases, but it is not possible to determine how typical these accounts were of the various patients that they were seeing. There are, however, some more comprehensive accounts detailing the case notes of every patient admitted to a particular institution during a particular period of time.

Gillian Doody studied the case notes of 337 male patients admitted to the Fife and Kinross District Asylum between 1874 and 1899. Although these notes were brief, Doody was able to assign each of the patients to one of four diagnostic categories: schizophrenia; affective disorder (disturbance of mood, as occurs in depression or mania); neurotic disorder (involving symptoms of stress or anxiety); and cases where there was a clear physical cause for the illness (such as a brain injury). According to Doody's classification, 10% of the patients were suffering from schizophrenia. Delusions, as identified by today's criteria, were present in 63% of the patients during their stay in the hospital. For example, 6% of delusions had a scientific theme, often referring to electricity, telegraphs, or flying machines. A religious preoccupation was evident in 18% of deluded patients. In the case of W. B., a 22-year-old man, restraint was required to prevent him going to London to be 'turned into an angel'. Alexander B. was described as standing in a grotesque attitude as if praying, consequent upon his firm belief that the Spirit of God was within him. Delusions of persecution were reported for over one-third of those recorded as being deluded. Many patients had the belief that they were going to be poisoned by substances such as hemlock, laudanum, chloroform, or brimstone. Others described being mesmerized and meddled with by occult forces, or 'haunted by the balloon folk'. One patient attempted to escape from the asylum because of his belief that he was being pursued by 'humphy-backed buggers with eyes like bulls'.

It is not possible to gain a clearer impression of what the experience of these patients was really like because detailed descriptions are not found in records of this type. However, over the last 25 years one of us, Eve Johnstone, has been directly involved in several large studies on groups of patients at varying stages in their illness. These studies span the period from 1909 to 1990. Notes from the studies provide a glimpse of the dramatic changes in the lives of patients diagnosed with schizophrenia during the course of the 20th century.

The era before drug treatment, 1930s–1960s

Before the discovery of antipsychotic drugs (neuroleptics) there were no effective treatments for schizophrenia. Antipsychotic drugs were introduced into psychiatry in 1952, and they were in general use by the 1960s (see Chapter 4). However, these drugs were not used everywhere. In the 1970s, David Owens and Eve Johnstone surveyed the entire population of patients (1,227 in number) resident in Shenley Hospital. This was a large psychiatric hospital north of London, which has since closed. Of these patients, 510 met standard criteria for a diagnosis of schizophrenia and were assessed in great detail, including recording all the physical treatments that they had ever received. It was found that 65 of these patients had never been prescribed antipsychotic drugs. This was because, at that time, Shenley Hospital was divided into two sides corresponding to the two London boroughs which it served. The consultants on one side had orthodox views and their patients had

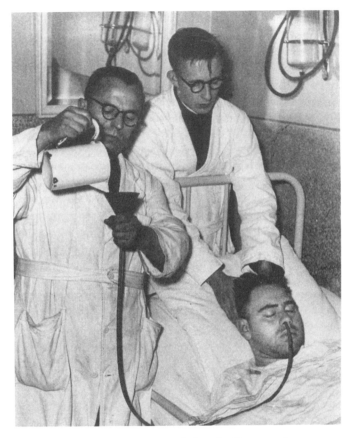

2. Insulin coma therapy: treatment before the discovery of antipsychotic drugs. In this type of therapy, the patient was given increasingly large doses of the hormone insulin, which reduces the sugar content of the blood, to produce a state of coma. The patient was kept in a comatose condition for about an hour, after which time they were brought back to consciousness by administration of a warm sugar solution via a stomach tube or by intravenous injection of glucose.

received a full range of the treatments usual at the time, including insulin coma therapy (see Figure 2), electroconvulsive shock therapy (application of an electric current to the brain to produce seizures), and antipsychotic drugs.

The other side of the hospital was supervised by consultants who were influenced by the idea of the 'therapeutic community' that was fashionable in the 1960s. These consultants did not prescribe antipsychotic drugs. When we arrived, we were surprised that some of the relatively young patients who had not had antipsychotic drugs nevertheless showed extreme withdrawal and bizarre, repetitive movements – at the time many people believed that such behaviour was actually caused by the drug treatment (see Chapter 4).

Detailed notes about some of these cases are still available. In one particularly striking example, one of the patients, on being asked what was wrong, appeared to say 'it's the place on my shoulder'. When asked what the problem was with the place, he said 'it's the place, the place, they gave me cream to put on it, how could that possibly help?'. Then asked to expand on this, he said 'How could cream help a fish, it's a fish, it's the place, not P-L-A-C-E but the P-L-A-I-C-E on my shoulder, it's there all the time'. This man seemed to go about his day-to-day affairs in the ward, reasonably happily, dressed normally, and could conduct a conversation on everyday matters reasonably appropriately. Nonetheless, he expressed the belief that there was a fish on his shoulder all the time. How the play on words between place and plaice came into all of this we could not determine.

3. Shenley Hospital: the grounds and a day room.

The following cases give us some idea of what it was like to have schizophrenia before treatment with drugs became ubiquitous.

Case 1

This patient was born in 1911 and was admitted to Shenley Hospital on Christmas Eve 1935, when he was 24. Assessments were done 39 years later, in 1975. He had never left hospital during that time. There is no record of him ever having been given antipsychotic drugs or any other physical treatment. He had left school at 14 and had worked as a wireless assistant before he became ill. He showed many features typical of schizophrenia: he made repetitive and meaningless movements; he spoke to himself and behaved in ways that suggested he was hearing voices, and sometimes reported hearing voices addressing him. He also showed negative features of schizophrenia. He said little and was sometimes mute for long periods. During one 15-minute interview he uttered only three words. He had lost interest in all activities and neglected his appearance. He would stand or sit for hours in the same position, and at times he adopted bizarre postures of his arms and legs. From time to time, he would smile incongruously. He had no visitors.

Case 6

This patient was born in 1911 and was admitted to Shenley Hospital in 1935 at the age of 24. He was seen in 1974, by which time he had been an in-patient for 39 years. He had never been treated with antipsychotic drugs. Before he became ill, he had worked as a professional violinist in a well-known dance band of the time and could still be persuaded to talk about this. He would describe how he had done a tour of the Astoria Ballrooms throughout Britain the year before he was admitted to hospital. On one occasion, he brought with him his violin, which he normally kept in a case under his bed. After some prompting, he played dance tunes that had been part of his repertoire when he was working. He played these accurately, and quite well, although in a slow, drawn-out style, which may well have been popular in the 1930s. He reported that thoughts were inserted into his mind and also that he heard voices addressing him. He believed his thoughts could be read. He was noted to speak very little and to display incongruous emotions. During an interview in 1974, he did not talk spontaneously and showed little emotion, but he would reply appropriately if directly addressed. He persisted in the idea that his real age was 24, and said that this would always be the case however long he lived, a conviction he could not explain. During his time on the research ward he was visited by his mother. We learned that she had visited him every Friday since he was first admitted.

The era of institutionalization, 1930–1975

The cases described above are unusual in that the patients had not received treatment with antipsychotic drugs. However, they are typical of the era of institutionalization in that the patients had stayed in hospital for decades since the onset of their illness. At the time we began to study the patients in Shenley, it was widely believed that most of these patients did not need to be in hospital. We had expected that quite a few of the patients might not appear to have a great deal wrong with them. They might show mild withdrawal and apathy, but this might be the inevitable consequence of spending decades in hospital and being treated for years with antipsychotic drugs. In fact, we observed many serious problems. Only 32 of the 510 patients could be said to be relatively well. The problems experienced by the patients were various and affected their mental state, their intellectual capacities, their movements, and their general ability to behave in a manner that would have allowed them to lead independent lives in the outside world. We had expected that there would be quite a number who could have gone home with little further ado, had they a home to go

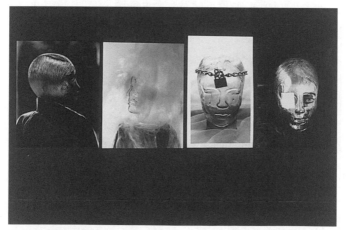

4. Chained by schizophrenia: from a series of photographs taken by the relative of a patient with schizophrenia.

to, but this really did not seem to be the case. These patients were obviously going to require continuing support if they were to leave hospital. Here are two illustrative examples.

Case 7

This man was born in 1923 and was admitted to Shenley Hospital in 1956 at the age of 33. He had received many physical treatments, including a prefrontal leucotomy (an operation to cut nerve fibres within the brain) and long-term treatment with antipsychotic drugs. At school he had shown outstanding artistic ability, but he did not achieve any leaving certificates. He worked as a commercial artist before he became ill. In his notes it is stated that in the immediate post-war period he earned over £1,000 a year, at that time a very comfortable salary. On admission in 1956 he believed that he was being persecuted and that alien forces were controlling his actions. He sometimes spoke incoherently and showed a loss of interest. When he was examined in May 1975, by which time he had been continuously in hospital for 23 years, he still reported many of these positive features. He heard people talking to him and about him; he heard his thoughts spoken aloud and believed that forces were trying to control his actions; he said that although the voices came from parts of his body, they were nothing to do with him. He talked freely and at length with an extensive vocabulary, but at times used words in an idiosyncratic way and occasionally became incoherent so that meaningful communication was impossible. He showed little sign of negative features. He spent much of his time pacing up and down aimlessly, but was able to concentrate on television programmes and discussed these with a show of interest and warmth.

Case 8

This man was born in 1928 and was admitted to Shenley Hospital at the age of 22. He had left school at 14 and had worked as a tea boy and then as a builder's labourer. His mother had died in a mental hospital when he was six years old. He received long-term treatment with antipsychotic drugs. He heard people talking about him and heard his thoughts being spoken aloud. He believed that he was being persecuted and that people were trying to control his actions. Sometimes he spoke little and lacked emotional responses, while at other times he became over-excited, occasionally throwing and breaking things. When examined in 1975 he still reported many of these positive features. He complained that there was a coil oscillating which made noises that disturbed his mind, and considered that he was being affected by bizarre physical forces that were controlling his body. He was sometimes incoherent, but most of the time it was possible to understand the meaning that he wished to convey. He did not show negative features. He looked after himself, conversed spontaneously, and took some interest in his surroundings.

The era of de-institutionalization, 1975–1985

In the 1970s it came to be widely believed that patients with schizophrenia would be much better off if they were not kept for decades in large institutions. It was thought that long-term institutional care could, by itself, produce apathy, social withdrawal, and deterioration in personal habits. In Chapter 6 we shall return to this idea and consider to what extent these features are a result of institutionalization or a consequence of schizophrenia. As is clear from the cases presented so far, apathy and social withdrawal were often seen in patients in the large asylums. Because of these ideas about institutionalization, policy towards patients with schizophrenia was already beginning to change. Where possible, new patients were kept in hospital for only short periods of time.

What happened to those patients who were sent back into the community rather than being kept in hospital? We interviewed 80 patients with a diagnosis of schizophrenia who had been discharged from Shenley Hospital during the early 1970s. Some of these people were well, and functioning successfully in the community. It was a pleasure to see how good a recovery they had made. Others had many difficulties and disabilities, and they and their relatives were under great strain. Here are some cases illustrating the range of levels of functioning we observed among this group.

Functioning well

This lady had no medical or social support and regarded herself as requiring none. She was a 28-year-old single woman who lived with her foster mother between engagements as a highly successful nightclub dancer in Europe and North America. Neither she nor her foster mother reported any problems. She was lively and charming. The foster mother was proud of her exotic and prosperous daughter and, indeed, grateful to her for the financial help that she provided.

Possible problems

This 47-year-old man lived with his wife and baby daughter and worked as a booking clerk. He and his wife stated that there were difficulties at home because of his excessive irritability and anxiety. At interview, he was strikingly anxious and described a preoccupation with spiritualism. This was unusual, not something that would have been expected in his cultural context, but it could not unequivocally be said to be abnormal.

Definite problems

This 58-year-old housewife lived with her 59-year-old husband and 22-year-old son. She believed that they were poisoning her. She cooked and shopped for herself alone and would not be in the same room with either member of her family. She shouted at night to hallucinations and was abusive to any visitors who called. At interview, she would not reply to any questions. Her dress was brightly coloured and unusual in a way that would have been regarded as bizarre by the average onlooker. She was surrounded by ornaments, principally snow-storm toys which appeared to be of symbolic significance to her. She showed inappropriate emotions and, although she spoke only briefly, it was clear that her speech was often incoherent.

The cases we have just described come from the era of 'care in the community'. That is to say, they were discharged from hospital promptly following assessment and treatment, and they returned home, although often continuing to attend a day centre. There has been much discussion in the medical and the national press of the success or otherwise of 'care in the community'. We were involved in a large-scale follow-up study of patients with schizophrenia who were discharged into the community between 1975 and 1985. This was an interesting study for us to conduct because we had the opportunity to see for ourselves exactly what had happened to patients who had been under our care many years before. On the whole, the patients' lives had not been easy – recurring symptoms and repeated admissions were usual. Some of the patients were dead. Many were unemployed and experienced other social difficulties, and a distressingly high proportion had tried to harm themselves. A minority were coping well with their symptoms, or were symptom-free, and leading happy, successful lives.

The frequent occurrence of self-harm, suicide, and early death is a disturbing finding of this study. Aspects of their behaviour had brought more than 30% of those interviewed into contact with the police, although there were only 10 offences involving behaviour actually or potentially dangerous to other people, with one offence resulting in death. This is rather less in the way of violent crime than might have been anticipated from the stories in the popular press mentioned at the beginning of this chapter.

The onset of schizophrenia

Almost all the patients we have described so far had been ill for many years. The condition of these people is inevitably coloured by their experiences subsequent to their illness. So, between 1979 and 1982, Fiona MacMillan assessed a large number of patients who were experiencing their first episode of schizophrenia. We reproduce some of her vignettes here to show how diverse this disorder can be.

Case 38

This man was a 31-year-old honours graduate. Two years before he became unwell he had organized and obtained funds for a rehabilitation project for unemployed youths. A year before his admission, he tried to kill himself by poison and then left work (in which he was regarded as highly successful) of his own volition. Some months later, he came to hospital with widespread delusions, which were, however, expressed with considerable incoherence. He described positive energy being used to achieve freedom for people, transmission of thought, an alternative universe, and the fleeting belief that he could fly. He had many visual misperceptions, and he felt that his head was being moved by alien forces. He was perplexed, but remained calm. After drug treatment his delusions and misperceptions largely ceased, but he remained vague. After two years, he was still unemployed and lacking in motivation.

Case 177

This 27-year-old man from a pleasant working-class family was reported to have changed from his usual self on return from a holiday seven years previously. Since that time, he had become increasingly erratic in his employment. Two years prior to admission, he had refused to attend the Department of Social Security to collect his unemployment benefit and had refused to see any medical personnel. He became restless and distracted, refused to wash or change his clothes, and began to grimace and smile inappropriately. On admission, he was dishevelled and was markedly lacking in emotion, with bouts of incongruous grimacing. He said he could see his face changing into that of a woman and believed that his thoughts were available to others due to his special powers of telepathic communication. He periodically believed that others followed him and spied upon him, but was reluctant to discuss this. He contradicted himself when discussing auditory hallucinations, but he clearly described visual hallucinations of solid cartoon characters and was troubled by a persistent feeling of a presence trying to take him over. He attended day care for 80 weeks and was still not well at the end of the study.

Case 232

The most striking feature of this 20-year-old woman was her very disorganized behaviour in the initial interview. She would sit for only moments in a chair and then wander round the room, picking up articles and occasionally sitting on the floor. Her limited spontaneous speech often consisted of abrupt commands to be given something. It was almost impossible to gain her attention. She repeatedly removed her dressing gown and made inappropriate sexual advances to the male staff, then tore bits off a picture of a swan. She appeared neither depressed nor elated and moved slowly. She said that God talked to her, saying 'shut up and get out of here' when replying to an enquiry about interference with her thinking. The patient said 'the thoughts go back to the swan, I want the cross to keep it forever and ever. It depends on the soldier, Marcus the nurse'. After six months in hospital, this patient returned to her mother's home, and 14 months later remained there, attending a day centre. She was withdrawn, lethargic, and without motivation and showed little emotion and sometimes adopted incongruous postures. Before her illness, she had left home, living independently, and had been contemplating marriage.

Case 240

This 19-year-old young woman was initially almost unable to cooperate with the interview at all because of her overwhelming distress. She described how something strange had happened to her that she could not understand. Colours of ordinary articles had become much too vivid and bright, and her face had changed into that of a rabbit with ears and whiskers while she watched in the mirror. She heard the voices of her dead grandfather, her mother, and her fiancé. The voices kept her awake at night questioning her, saying 'who are you?' and occasionally discussing her relations with her fiancé in a most personal and distressing fashion. She had hallucinations of being touched in a sexual manner, and she believed that reference had been made to her engagement in the mass media. After four months she returned home but remained lethargic and somewhat emotionally brittle. She was readily distressed by mention of her illness. She married her fiancé some six months later, and 14 months after the admission remained out of hospital with no hallucinations and delusions. She was said to be rather more dependent and child-like than she had been prior to her illness.

From the cases we have described it is clear that schizophrenia is diverse and is associated with bizarre, inexplicable, and frightening experiences and with behaviour that is strange and difficult to understand. The experiences described by sufferers today are very similar to those described in the past. It is easy to understand why accounts of this illness elicit fear, but, rather, they should elicit sympathy. To quote again from the first case in this chapter: 'I cannot picture anything more frightful than for a well-endowed cultivated human being to live through his own gradual deterioration fully aware of it all the time.'

Chapter 2
The concept of schizophrenia

The development of the concept

Madness (or what we now call mental disorder) has been recognized and studied since medical records began, although the terms psychosis and schizophrenia are of rather recent origin. Psychosis is any severe form of mental disorder in which the patient has lost touch with reality. Schizophrenia is one of the major examples of psychotic illness. A patient suffering from psychosis has lost touch with reality in the sense that he or she believes things that cannot possibly be true (delusions) or hears voices and sees visions when there are no sensory stimuli to create them (hallucinations).

Ancient Egyptian and Greek texts describe people with hallucinations,

> in some cases the girl [said] dreadful things: [the visions ordered] her to jump up and throw herself into wells and drown, as if this were good for her and served a useful purpose
>
> Hippocrates

and delusions,

> The patient may imagine he has taken another form than his own.

One believes himself a God, orator or actor, carrying gravely a stalk
of straw and imagining himself holding a sceptre of the World.

Aretaeus

However, many of the terms that were used then to describe mental
illness later acquired rather different meanings, so that ancient
systems for classifying mental disorders were not the same as those
used today. For example, the term 'mania' was more or less
equivalent to a frenzied form of madness, rather than referring
specifically to elated mood as it does now. Aretaeus (*c.* AD 150–200)
considered that sorrow and dejection were essential elements of
melancholia, but this disorder also involved delusions – 'The
melancholic isolates himself, he is afraid of being persecuted and
imprisoned.' Aretaeus also observed how an acute attack of mental
illness could be followed by a dramatic deterioration of function:

> There are patients suffering from a serious form of mania, who after
> an illness become insensitive; their intelligence degrades, they
> forget themselves and spend the rest of their lives like brutes.

There was little progress in the understanding of mental disorders
during the Middle Ages. Approaches to mental disorders in
medieval Europe closely followed the tradition left by Aretaeus and
his contemporary, Galen (AD 130–199). A hospital for the care of the
insane was founded in the 13th century in London, and in England
the lunacy legislation dates from 1320, but detailed classification
and description of mental disorders, in Britain and in Europe as a
whole, did not begin until the end of the 18th century. At that time,
mental disorders were divided roughly into four categories: idiocy
(intellectual impairment present from early in life); dementia
(intellectual impairment acquired later in life); mania (insanity
associated with many delusions and disturbed behaviour); and
melancholia (insanity associated with circumscribed delusions and
social withdrawal).

In 1794, Philippe Pinel commenced work at the Bicêtre Hospital in

Paris, and published the study *Traité de la manie*, which distinguished between mania with and without delirium, in 1801. His ideas were followed up by Esquirol, who developed a lecture course and wrote a textbook of psychiatry published in 1838, introducing the concept of monomania:

> The patients seize upon a false principle, which they pursue without deviating from logical reasonings, and from which they deduce legitimate consequences, which modify their affections, and the acts of their will. Aside from this partial delirium, they think, reason and act like other men.

It was in Germany that psychiatry first became established as a subject for academic study in the universities, Heinroth being appointed to the first Chair of Mental Therapy in Leipzig in 1811. Griesinger was appointed the first Professor of Psychiatry and Neurology in Berlin in 1865, where he developed a department for the study of mental disorders. Work there was based upon the hypothesis that 'mental illness is a somatic illness of the brain'.

The theme of the relationship of mental disorder to brain abnormality (neuropathology) was pursued in a particularly successful way in relation to what we would now recognize as neurosyphilis (then termed general paralysis of the insane). This was shown to be a single disease that presented as a sequence of clinical syndromes. The patient first appeared as manic and ambitious, then as melancholic and hypochondriacal, and finally as demented. The order of appearance of these syndromes depended on the progress of lesions in the brain. Neuropathological approaches to dementia were also successful. For example, Carl Wernicke published a description of the brain disorder named after him in 1881 (Wernicke's encephalopathy – a condition resulting in mental confusion that is caused by a dietary deficiency of the B vitamin thiamine, usually associated with excessive alcohol consumption). In 1907, Alois Alzheimer reported characteristic neuropathological changes in the brain of a 51-year-old woman with intellectual impairment and psychotic features – the first description of the condition subsequently called Alzheimer's disease. However, there was still a large class of severe mental illnesses for which no characteristic brain pathology could be detected. These were termed 'functional' psychoses.

Kraepelin introduces the concept of dementia praecox

It was against this background of relating neuropathology to clinical features that Emil Kraepelin developed his ideas about mental disorders. He wrote nine editions of his *Lehrbuch der Psychiatrie* [Textbook of Psychiatry] between 1893 and 1927.

In the earlier editions, he described the unsatisfactory nature of the diagnostic categories that had been used in the earlier part of the 19th century. He regarded these as being unhelpful, particularly for predicting the course and outcome of a mental disorder. In the fourth and fifth editions of the *Lehrbuch*, Kraepelin created a new classification system and clarified his diagnostic ideas. He went beyond straightforward clinical description and divided the broad class of functional psychosis into two categories, essentially on the basis of outcome. The first category, which he called manic-depressive insanity, pursued a fluctuating course with frequent relapses but with full recovery between episodes. The second, for which he used Morel's term dementia praecox, embraced catatonia (as described by Kahlbaum), hebephrenia (as described by Hecker), and his own dementia paranoides, as described in the table below (p. 29).

Kraepelin grouped these together as different manifestations of a progressive disease that either pursued a steady downhill course to a state of chronic impairment or, if improvement did occur, resulted in only partial recovery. He believed that the cluster of symptoms and signs that had the characteristic course and outcome of

5. **Emil Kraepelin (1856–1926) created the concept of schizophrenia, which he called dementia praecox. This picture dates from about 1887, when Kraepelin was director of the psychiatric clinic of the University of Dorpat in Tartu, Estonia.**

dementia praecox had a specific pathology in the brain and a specific cause, even though essentially nothing was known of either the pathology or the cause during his lifetime. The symptoms that he emphasized included auditory and tactile hallucinations, delusions, incoherent speech, blunted emotions, negativism (resisting suggestions and doing the opposite), stereotyped

Table 1 The three syndromes that formed the basis for
Kraepelin's concept of dementia praecox

Syndrome	Explanation	Signs and symptoms
Catatonia (insanity with abnormal muscle tone)	immobility	reduced movement
	mutism/alogia	reduced speech
	negativism	resistance to instructions
	staring	reduced eye movements
	stereotypies	pointless, repetitive movements
	verbigeration	pointless, repetitive speech
	echolalia	imitation of speech of others
	echopraxia	imitation of gestures of others
Hebephrenia (adolescent insanity)	delusions	false beliefs
	hallucinations	false perceptions
	disorganized speech	–
	disorganized behaviour	–
	anhedonia	inability to feel pleasure
	abulia/avolition	loss of motivation
	bizarre affect	inappropriate emotional responses
Dementia paranoides (Delusional insanity with declining course)	delusions	false beliefs

behaviour, and lack of insight. Nonetheless, he appreciated that the condition was diverse and difficult to classify. He wrote,

> The presentation of clinical details in the large domain of dementia praecox meets with considerable difficulties because a delineation of the different clinical pictures can only be accomplished artificially. There is certainly a whole series of phases which frequently return but between them are such numerous transitions that, in spite of all efforts, it appears impossible at present to delimit them sharply and to assign each case without objection to a different form.

Bleuler coins the term schizophrenia

While Kraepelin was still defining and clarifying his concept in the successive editions of his *Lehrbuch*, Bleuler published his *Dementia Praecox or the Group of Schizophrenias*.

Although he apparently considered that he was developing Kraepelin's concept, his ideas were, in fact, not at all the same. He was influenced by the ideas currently being developed by Freud and saw schizophrenia in terms very different from the neuropathological ones envisaged by Kraepelin. His term schizophrenia, meaning split mind, was intended to describe a loosening of the associations between the different functions of the mind so that thoughts became disconnected and coordination between emotional, cognitive, and volitional processes became weaker. He considered that ambivalence (the presence of conflicting emotions and desires); autism (lack of social contact); abulia, or avolition (loss of will); and abnormal affectivity (bizarre or blunted emotional responses) were fundamental features that could be observed in every case and that the hallucinations, delusions, catatonic features, and other elements of behavioural disturbance emphasized by Kraepelin were secondary phenomena which might or might not be present.

In Bleuler's view, the diagnosis of schizophrenia could be made even

6. Eugen Bleuler (1857–1939) coined the term schizophrenia.

when delusions or hallucinations had never been present at any time. On the basis of that idea, he added to the catatonic, paranoid, and hebephrenic forms of illness described by Kraepelin latent and simple subtypes of schizophrenia. Bleuler's ideas became influential in the United States, but in Europe Kraepelin's concept of dementia praecox, even although that term was replaced by schizophrenia, continued to dominate diagnostic habits. As a result, different diagnostic practices developed on the two sides of the Atlantic.

How should schizophrenia be diagnosed?

Bleuler's concept of schizophrenia as an essentially psychological disorder, possibly with a psychogenic basis, rather than a pathological condition of the nervous system was attractive to psychiatrists in the United States. This view fitted in well with the psychoanalytical tradition that prevailed there until the 1970s. As a result, psychiatrists in the United States had a very broad concept of schizophrenia, one that included patients who in the United Kingdom would have been regarded as having depressive or manic psychoses, or even as suffering from non-psychotic neurotic states or personality disorders. Indeed, in the United States from the 1950s, the concept of 'pseudoneurotic schizophrenia' was employed; patients could be regarded as having a form of schizophrenia on the basis of a wide range of neurotic symptoms such as phobias, obsessions, and depersonalization (a feeling of detachment from one's self, like being an automaton). These symptoms were often associated with severe anxiety and attacks of 'psychotic disturbance lasting days, hours or perhaps only minutes'.

In 1972, the US/UK diagnostic project demonstrated that the diagnosis of schizophrenia was very much more frequently employed in the United States than in the United Kingdom. In a series of 250 cases in New York, 62% of patients were given a hospital diagnosis of schizophrenia, whereas in the London series the proportion was only 34%. However, when the same patients were diagnosed using a standardized procedure (International

Classification of Diseases) the proportions were much more similar, at 29% and 35%, respectively. By contrast, 32% of the London sample received a hospital diagnosis of manic-depressive disorder, but only 5% of the New York sample were given such a diagnosis. It was evident that the concept of schizophrenia in New York was much wider than that employed in London.

The development of standard diagnostic criteria

Following upon the findings of the US/UK diagnostic project, there was widespread acceptance of the idea that standardized methods of reaching a diagnosis were required. There had already been some attempts to provide such methods, notably the Diagnostic and Statistical Manual (DSM) of the American Psychiatric Association of 1952 and the Glossary of the 8th Revision of the International Classification of Diseases (ICD), but these were of limited value because they simply provided descriptions of the typical features of each condition, giving no indication of how less than typical cases should be classified. A considerable advance was the development of operational definitions that provided a set of clearly defined criteria that had to be fulfilled. In the last quarter of the 20th century several such schemes were developed and these continue to be widely used. In these schemes the diagnosis of schizophrenia has generally been applied only when the patient shows psychotic features, that is delusions, hallucinations, and/or thought disorder. In his original formulation of the schizophrenias, Bleuler had included the concepts of latent and simple schizophrenia. Since such patients do not show psychotic symptoms, they would not receive a diagnosis of schizophrenia under current diagnostic schemes.

At the present time, the most widely used definitions of schizophrenia, at least in research practice, are the St Louis Criteria, the Research Diagnostic Criteria, the World Health Organization's ICD-10, and the American Psychiatric Association DSM-IV (see the box below).

DSM-IV criteria for a diagnosis of schizophrenia

A. *Characteristic symptoms*: Two (or more) of the following, each present for a significant portion of time during a one-month period (or less if successfully treated):

(i) delusions

(ii) hallucinations

(iii) disorganized speech (e.g. frequent derailment or incoherence)

(iv) grossly disorganized or catatonic behaviour

(v) negative symptoms, i.e. affective flattening, alogia, or avolition

Note: Only one Criterion A symptom is required if delusions are bizarre or hallucinations consist of a voice keeping up a running commentary on the person's behaviour or thoughts, or two or more voices conversing with each other.

B: *Social/occupational dysfunction*: For a significant portion of the time since the onset of the disturbance, one or more major areas of functioning such as work, interpersonal relations, or self-care are markedly below the level achieved prior to the onset.

C: *Duration*: Continuous signs of the disturbance persist for at least six months. This six-month period must include at least one month of symptoms (or less if successfully treated) that meet Criterion A.

D: *Exclusion of mood disorders*: No major episodes of depression or elation have occurred concurrently with the psychotic symptoms.

E: *Exclusion of known organic causes*: The disturbance is not due to the direct effect of drugs (a drug of abuse or a side-effect of medication) or a known brain disorder (e.g. a brain tumour).

These systems all have a great deal in common. They all require clear evidence of psychosis (hallucinations, delusions, thought disorder), occurring currently or in the past, and all but the St Louis Criteria specify particular kinds of hallucinations or delusions. All four systems require that affective (emotional) symptoms are not prominent and specify a minimum duration of illness, but this is only two weeks for the Research Diagnostic Criteria definition, one month for ICD-10, and six months for St Louis and DSM-IV.

First-rank symptoms of schizophrenia

In all the diagnostic systems we have mentioned so far a diagnosis of schizophrenia cannot be made solely on the basis of the presence of certain symptoms (hallucinations and delusions). In addition, the symptoms have to have been present for a significant period of time and there has to be evidence of decline in social function. A different approach is used in the Present State Examination (PSE Catego system). This scheme relies upon a detailed standardized interview of the patient to elicit signs and symptoms and does not incorporate other information about illness duration, past functioning, family history, and so on. Scores from the interview are fed into a computer program called Catego. To arrive at a diagnosis of schizophrenia, the Catego program operates on the idea that if certain symptoms are present (so-called nuclear schizophrenic symptoms) then the diagnosis will be one of schizophrenia – to use an analogy from contract bridge, nuclear symptoms are always trumps. These nuclear symptoms were selected on the basis of the work done by Kurt Schneider in defining the central features of the disorder. Schneider described a number of 'features of first rank' whose presence he considered to be pathognomonic (characteristic) of schizophrenia, provided that obvious brain disease was not present. Schneider's features of the first rank are shown in the following table.

Many of these experiences can be interpreted as a result of the

Table 2 Schneider's first-rank symptoms (from Mellors, 1970)

Audible thoughts	The patient would think 'I must put the kettle on' and after a pause of not more than one second the voice would say 'I must put the kettle on'.
Voices arguing	One voice said 'GT is a bloody paradox', another said 'He is that, he should be locked up', while a third interrupted 'He is not, he is a lovely man'.
Voices commenting on one's actions	The voice went on in a flat monotone describing everything the patient was doing. 'She is peeling potatoes, got hold of the peeler, she does not want that potato'.
Influence playing on the body (somatic passivity)	'X-rays enter the back of my neck, where the skin tingles and feels warm, they pass down the back in a hot tingling strip about six inches wide to the waist.'
Thought withdrawal	'I am thinking about my mother, and suddenly my thoughts are sucked out of my mind by a phrenological vacuum extractor, and there is nothing in my mind.'
Thought insertion	'The thoughts of Eamonn Andrews come into my mind. He treats my mind like a screen and flashes his thoughts on to it like you flash a picture.'

Schizophrenia

Thought broadcasting	'My thoughts leave my head on a type of mental ticker-tape. Everyone around me has only to pass the tape through their mind and they know my thoughts.'
'Made' feelings	'It is not me who is unhappy, but they are projecting unhappiness into my brain. They project upon me laughter for no reason.'
'Made' impulses	'It came to me from the X-ray department. It was nothing to do with me, they wanted it so I picked up the bottle and poured it.'
'Made' volitional acts (delusions of control)	'It is my hand and arm that move, and my fingers pick up the pen, but I don't control them. What they do is nothing to do with me.'
Delusional perception	One of the lodgers pushed the salt cellar towards him and the patient knew that he must return home, 'To greet the Pope who is visiting Ireland to see his family and reward them'.

failure to distinguish between ideas and impulses arising from within the subject's own mind and perceptions arising from stimuli in the external world, but for Schneider their importance lay in their value as a practical guide to diagnosis. The idea was that if any one of these symptoms was clearly present in the absence of organic brain disease, then the diagnosis could be considered to be that of schizophrenia. He accepted that some patients with schizophrenia never exhibited these symptoms, and that all of them could, at times, occur in organic psychoses, but he considered that it was useful to distinguish them from what he called symptoms of the second rank, for example perplexity, emotional blunting, and hallucinations and delusions of other kinds. The selection of nuclear symptoms in the PSE Catego system was much influenced by Schneider's ideas.

It is far from unusual for a patient to receive a diagnosis of schizophrenia from application of one of these standardized schemes, but not from another. For example, a patient who experienced first-rank symptoms for a very short time would receive a diagnosis of schizophrenia from the PSE, but not from DSM-IV. All these definitions are arbitrary and are justified only by their usefulness. These definitions are useful because they provide reliability and, in research terms particularly, this is important. The readers of a medical study will know what is meant by a diagnosis of schizophrenia if one of the standardized schemes was employed. The difficulties demonstrated by the US/UK Diagnostic Project can be avoided.

Reliability in itself, however, may be no great advantage. Within a framework of strict rules it should always be possible to achieve a reliable diagnosis, but accuracy of diagnosis also depends on the quality of the information acquired from the psychiatric interview. Most of the features upon which the diagnosis of schizophrenia is made depend upon introspective reports from the patient. In response to the same direct question, a patient with auditory hallucinations may deny that he hears voices to a series of interviewers; 100% reliability of diagnosis can be achieved, but it is possible for it to be based in every case upon misinformation. The specific types of psychotic symptoms necessary to fulfil operational definitions of schizophrenia can usually be described in such a way that there is no great difficulty in making a decision about their presence or absence, or indeed in grading their severity. Nevertheless, we have no alternative but to depend upon the veracity of the patient's statement in this respect. Eve Johnstone has interviewed over 4,000 individuals thought to have schizophrenia, of whom only a handful gave accounts of themselves which subsequent events demonstrated to be untrue. Nevertheless, that small number of individuals could mislead an experienced psychiatrist into giving a wholly erroneous diagnosis. This is rare, but it is important not to lose sight of the limitations of reliability and to bear in mind that standardized diagnostic procedures do not eliminate the need for skilled and experienced clinicians.

Is the diagnosis of schizophrenia associated with a poor outcome?

Quite distinct from the question of reliability of diagnosis is the question of validity. Does the diagnosis of schizophrenia predict some important variable such as a specific brain abnormality, response to treatment, or the likely outcome of the illness? Such validity was the justification that Kraepelin gave for introducing the concept of dementia praecox. From within the broad class of psychotic illnesses not associated with a demonstrable underlying brain lesion, he had set out to define a cluster of symptoms and signs that predicted a characteristically poor outcome. The facts were, however, that not all cases with this symptom cluster did have a poor outcome; in fact 13% of Kraepelin's own cases were said to have recovered. A frequent response to this problem was to try to redefine schizophrenia in terms of a slightly different cluster of clinical features in the hope that this new definition would provide better predictions of outcome. For example, in 1939 the Norwegian psychiatrist Langfeldt attempted to distinguish between patients who had true dementia praecox/schizophrenia and those who had what he called a schizophreniform psychosis. The idea behind this was that the study of schizophrenia was distorted because samples of patients included both genuine cases of the disorder and those who were superficially similar but who did not really have the condition.

These cases had a better outcome and did not actually have a tangible underlying disease process, so that investigations for such a process would always be negative. This was an appealing idea, and Langfeldt presented evidence that was not methodologically strong but which indicated that true 'process schizophrenia' and schizophreniform psychoses had different outcomes and different responses to the physical treatments available at the time (electroconvulsive therapy and insulin coma therapy). It was also suggested that these 'lesser' psychoses superficially resembling schizophrenia but with a good outcome should be considered 'psychological' rather than 'physical' disorders – in other words, these disorders do not have abnormalities in the brain and are appropriately treated with psychotherapy. However, subsequent studies have not supported these ideas.

Poor outcome is still the variable most widely considered as a validating criterion for the diagnosis of schizophrenia. Outcome may be considered in terms of symptomatology (has the patient stopped experiencing the symptoms?) or in terms of social functioning (has the patient returned to the level of social functioning existing prior to the illness?). Studies have shown that operational definitions are more successful at predicting a poor symptomatic outcome than a poor social outcome, and, of course, as definitions for schizophrenia tend to include sustained duration of illness, such success is scarcely surprising. As far as most of medicine is concerned, there is no better predictor of what will happen in the future than examination of what has happened in the past. An illness that has been associated with six months of symptomatology of whatever kind is more likely to be associated with these symptoms in the future. For validation of the diagnosis of schizophrenia, it is more appropriate to use the PSE Catego system which considers only the patient's mental state at the time of the interview. In the International Pilot Study of Schizophrenia, which used this system, patients who were given a schizophrenic diagnosis had a worse outcome than those who received a non-schizophrenic diagnosis.

Another study relevant to this point is the Northwick Park Study of first episodes of schizophrenia. This used the PSE Catego system to identify cases of first episodes of schizophrenia. There are many practical difficulties in studying patients who are experiencing a psychotic illness for the first time: they are likely to be bewildered, frightened, and suspicious, and they will not have had time to develop a trusting relationship with the staff on the psychiatric ward. In the Northwick Park Study most of the examinations were conducted by Fiona MacMillan, often in circumstances that were less than ideal. Because they had only just met her, the patients were probably less able to be frank with her and were more suspicious of her than would otherwise have been the case.

Given all these difficulties in eliciting the precise symptoms experienced by the patients, and because we used the PSE rather than a diagnostic system that required a lengthy period of illness, it seemed likely that we would have included patients with brief psychotic episodes (rather than true schizophrenia) who would do well. In fact, this was not so. Outcome at two years in terms of symptoms and social functioning was far from encouraging. Only 13 of 253 patients made educational, occupational, or social achievements during that time. Clusters of symptoms used in the PSE to define schizophrenia did indeed appear to be associated with a poor outcome, even when these symptoms were detected under less than ideal circumstances.

The continuing search for validity

Kraepelin believed that schizophrenia (dementia praecox) was a disease and that, in due course, a tangible, physical marker of the underlying disease process would be found. The case of Alzheimer's disease provides an ideal scenario. First, characteristic physical markers (plaques and tangles) were found in the brains of affected patients, and subsequently (although it took nearly 100 years) specific genes have been identified for some cases. However, in spite of intensive research effort over many years, neither of these events has occurred for schizophrenia. In the absence of validation through some physical marker, the definition of schizophrenia remains to some degree arbitrary. This is why there are slight differences between the standardized diagnostic schemes and why more radical suggestions for classification are proposed from time to time. For example, Tim Crow has proposed that Kraepelin's distinction between manic-depressive insanity and schizophrenia is not justified and that there is a better chance of finding neural markers for a unitary psychosis. The hope is that eventually a diagnostic scheme will be devised that 'cuts nature at the joints' more accurately. When this happens, we fondly imagine, everything will fall into place. Neural markers and gene markers will be revealed, and outcome and response to treatment will be accurately predicted.

How can a functional psychosis have an organic basis?

Against this background, the requirement in the standard diagnostic procedures that there be no evidence of organic brain disease is increasingly problematic. Kraepelin always assumed that there was some underlying abnormal physical process, but the syndromes he grouped together under the term dementia praecox were specifically disorders which, at that time, were not associated with any known brain disorder. Schneider considered that his symptoms could only be used to indicate a diagnosis of schizophrenia in the absence of obvious brain disease. In DSM-IV one of the necessary criteria (condition of exclusion E) states that, 'the disturbance is not due to the direct physiological effects of a substance (e.g. drug abuse and medication) or a general medical condition (i.e. a known physical disorder including brain damage)'. In spite of these strictures, investigators constantly search for physical abnormalities in patients with schizophrenia. Of course, we do not think that the physical abnormality will be a general medical condition of the type that is meant in the DSM-IV definition, but at some point we will have to decide whether a certain physical abnormality is a key feature of schizophrenia rather than an indication that the patient is suffering from some other disorder. There is a striking contrast here with the diagnosis of autism. This diagnosis is also based on a series of operational criteria describing various signs and symptoms. However, it is accepted that certain cases of autism may be associated with general medical conditions such as maternal rubella (German measles during pregnancy) or tuberous sclerosis (an obvious brain disease). Are we right to exclude patients with known brain disorders from the category of schizophrenia?

Where do we draw the line?

In many ways, the strength of the essentially Kraepelinian concept of schizophrenia in predicting poor outcome is unexpected because the foundations on which it rests all have their weaknesses. The diagnosis is generally only considered if patients are thought to have hallucinations and/or delusions. Firmly held delusions, commanding hallucinations, and incomprehensible speech are all easy to distinguish from normality. However, many patients experience only transient and partial forms of these symptoms. These borderline forms of hallucinations and delusions can be observed early in a schizophrenic illness and even in the normal population of young people.

The boundary between normality and psychosis is not clear-cut. It has been known for a long time that abnormal features can be observed before the onset of a clear-cut psychotic episode, and so it has generally been assumed that these transient or partial forms would always evolve into clear-cut and sustained psychotic features. However, this is not always the case. Even people experiencing repeated episodes of mildly psychotic symptoms may show no evidence of increasing severity of symptoms or any decline in social function. In our own work in the Edinburgh High Risk Study, we have observed people who have held ill-sustained but probably psychotic symptoms off and on for years without ever becoming floridly unwell, although, of course, we do not yet know what will happen to them in the long run.

There is more and more interest in what patients are like in the very early stages of the illness, or even before any illness is manifest. Studies of these very early stages might be able to answer questions about the mechanism by which a predisposed individual can switch from being relatively well to being clearly ill. More and more genetic studies are being conducted in which it is necessary to distinguish family members who are ill from those who are well. Should a narrow description be used to define the cases (he has had severe hallucinations and delusions for many years), or would a broad statement be more appropriate (he is a bit of a hippy)?

In particular, some studies employ the category of schizotypal personality disorder. Sometimes this personality disorder may evolve into overt schizophrenia, but usually it is a stable and enduring trait that is relatively common in the close relatives of people with schizophrenia and is assumed to be part of the genetic 'spectrum' of schizophrenia. DSM-IV criteria for this disorder are shown in the box.

It is evident that very different pictures emerge depending upon which five of the nine category A features are chosen. With one selection, those affected could have features that would amount to schizophrenia if somewhat more firmly held. With another selection, the picture might be quite familiar; many of us know people who seem a little eccentric, but are by no means insane. Where should we draw the line?

In practice most people diagnosed as having schizophrenia have a severe and enduring mental disorder that will persist or recur despite treatment. These people have obvious and persistent

DSM-IV criteria for schizotypal personality disorder

A. A pervasive pattern of social and interpersonal deficits marked by acute discomfort with, and reduced capacity for, close relationships as well as by cognitive or perceptual distortions and eccentricities of behaviour, beginning by early adulthood and present in a variety of contexts, as indicated by five (or more) of the following:

(i) ideas of reference (delusional belief that television or radio broadcasts refer to oneself, or that others are talking or thinking about oneself)

(ii) odd beliefs or magical thinking that influences behaviour and is inconsistent with subcultural norms (e.g. superstitiousness, belief in clairvoyance, telepathy, or 'sixth sense'; in children and adolescents, bizarre fantasies or preoccupations)

(iii) unusual perceptual experiences, including bodily illusions

(iv) odd thinking and speech (e.g. vague, circumstantial, metaphorical, over-elaborate, or stereotyped)

(v) suspiciousness or paranoid ideation

(vi) inappropriate or constricted affect

(vii) behaviour or appearance that is odd, eccentric, or peculiar

(viii) lack of close friends or confidants other than first-degree relatives

(ix) excessive social anxiety that does not diminish with familiarity and tends to be associated with paranoid fears rather than negative judgements about self

delusions and hallucinations and are no longer in touch with reality. The diagnostic line has been drawn here on the basis that such people will not be able to function in our society without considerable help.

The construct of schizophrenia has not changed much since Kraepelin's first proposal. His concept remains reasonably robust, but at its edges there are areas of uncertainty, and it is unlikely to be bettered until we have an understanding of the neural basis of the disorder.

Chapter 3

Intellectual functioning in schizophrenia

The dementia in dementia praecox

A key component in Kraepelin's formulation of dementia praecox was a decline in functioning. This, of course, is why he used the word dementia. As we have seen, a decline in functioning continues to be a requirement in most contemporary schemes for the diagnosis of schizophrenia. But what is the nature of this decline in function? Bleuler, apparently, disliked the name dementia praecox and felt that it was misleading since there was no dementia in the sense of senile dementia. Senile dementia is a decline in intellectual capacity associated with old age. Patients are typically disoriented (they cannot remember where they are or what time it is) and forgetful, and they have difficulty in finding words and in recognizing objects. This does not seem to be the kind of impairment Kraepelin had in mind. He described the dementia of dementia praecox as a 'dissolution of the personality' rather than as a decline in intellectual functioning. There is, he said, 'a weakening of those emotional activities which permanently form the mainspring of volition . . . the result . . . is emotional dullness, loss of mastery over volition, of endeavour, and of ability for independent action'.

His concept of 'dissolution' arose from ideas that were circulating at that time about the organization of the nervous system. This was thought to be composed of centres for 'lower' and 'higher' aspects of behaviour, so that reflexes were controlled by lower parts of the brain while the higher processes of the mind acted by influencing these lower mechanisms. There was a hierarchy of control such that each higher level exerted control over the lower one. However, the higher levels were held to be more fragile and thus more easily disrupted by temporary or permanent damage to the brain. This removal of control by the higher centres was characterized as a process of dissolution, the opposite of evolution. The effect of alcohol on the brain was thought to be an example of a temporary dissolution; Kraepelin had himself studied the effects of alcohol on psychological functions in experiments with normal volunteers.

So for Kraepelin the dementia associated with dementia praecox reflected dissolution of function in which higher mental centres no longer controlled lower levels, leading to 'loss of mastery over volition' and 'loss of ability for independent action'. Allowing for the difference in terminology, this sounds remarkably like a description of failure in what we would now call the 'central executive' – a high-level cognitive system for selecting and initiating appropriate actions to be carried out by lower-level 'slave' systems. As we shall see, this formulation of the core cognitive deficit associated with schizophrenia was reintroduced by neuropsychologists at the end of the 20th century. But first, we shall consider the evidence that general intellectual deficits can be found in people with a diagnosis of schizophrenia.

Schizophrenia and intelligence

A major concern in 20th-century psychology has been to define and measure intelligence. The concept of intelligence arises from the observation that intellectual abilities tend to be correlated. Someone who is good at mental arithmetic is, on balance, also likely to have a good vocabulary and to be good at problem solving. The best way of measuring this kind of general intelligence is to record performance on a wide range of different kinds of task. In many cases speed as well as accuracy is taken as a sign of good performance. Many intelligence (or IQ) tests of this kind have been developed, and information about performance on such tests is available from large samples of the general population. The most widely used is the Wechsler Adult Intelligence Scale (known as the WAIS). This test is designed so that the average score in the general population is 100 (that is, 50% of the general population will score at least 100 on the test), while the range of scores is such that about 70% of the general population will have IQs between 85 and 115. IQ scores show a marked decline in patients with dementia. A typical group of patients with dementia related to Alzheimer's disease will have an average IQ of around 80 and will show a decline of about 8 IQ points per year. When the same tests are used to measure intelligence in patients with schizophrenia, the average performance of the group is also well below the expected value of 100. In a study that we conducted of nearly 300 patients in the Harrow Health District the average IQ score was 93, compared to 111 in a group of patients suffering from neurotic disorders. Similar results have been obtained in many other studies.

Does intelligence decline in schizophrenia?

It is clear that patients with schizophrenia perform badly on intelligence tests, but what does this observation mean? It does not necessarily indicate a decline in intelligence, since it is possible that these patients would have performed badly on IQ tests even before they became ill. But there are certainly some cases in which there has been an obvious decline in function. Patients with a diagnosis of schizophrenia often fail to fulfil their academic promise, as is illustrated on page 50.

However, there are also cases in which the patient has clearly never functioned at a normal level. In the histories of the long-stay patients at Shenley Hospital, rather more than would be expected were said never to have functioned very well. It is possible that

> An academically gifted public schoolboy went to Oxford to study classics; initially he appeared to be doing very well and was thought likely to gain a first-class degree. But in the second year, he became more withdrawn and in the third, obviously psychotic. He gradually recovered with treatment but was not able to return to Oxford. He transferred to a provincial university, changed to a history course, and did achieve a pass degree. He obtained a post as an assistant in a university library, but could not do it. After some time he got a post as a shelf stacker in a supermarket, but could not do this either, and thereafter he was unemployed. He would often go to libraries to take out history books, but said he was never able to concentrate on them or complete them.

many patients with schizophrenia perform badly on IQ tests even before they become ill. The problem is that in most cases we do not have IQ test scores from a time prior to the onset of the illness. In certain countries it is possible to find records of intelligence test scores from some years prior to the first episode of schizophrenia. This is the case in Israel. By law, Israeli males between the ages of 16 and 17 are summoned by the Draft Board for screening prior to military service. This screening includes a psychiatric assessment, tests of cognitive ability, and a behavioural assessment. From a sample of about 13,000 such Draft Board records, Rabinowitz and his colleagues were able to identify 692 males who had also received a hospital diagnosis of schizophrenia. They also identified a large number of suitably matched control records. The time of onset of the first episode of schizophrenia varied from up to one year before testing to eight years later. The results are clear-cut and lead to two conclusions. First, the young men who subsequently developed schizophrenia had lower scores on an intelligence test by about 5 IQ points. Second, the impairment became greater as the time of testing occurred closer to the first episode. Young men who had already been diagnosed with schizophrenia prior to testing scored about 15 IQ points below the controls. Clearly people with a diagnosis of schizophrenia perform less well on IQ tests than they did prior to the onset of their illness and therefore show a decline in performance. However, in many cases IQ test performance was lower than average long before the onset of the illness. Very similar results have been obtained in studies in which premorbid IQ has been estimated on the basis of current test performance.

Is treatment the cause of poor performance on IQ tests?

It is clear that people with a diagnosis of schizophrenia perform badly on tests of intelligence, but this need not be a direct consequence of the illness. It could be a consequence of the way the illness is treated. For most of the 20th century people with schizophrenia remained for very long periods, and often for life, in large institutions that were frequently deliberately isolated from the community. Even in the best cases the environment in these institutions was clearly impoverished. We shall discuss the effects of this institutionalization further in Chapter 6.

There are a number of ways of deciding whether or not the impairment in IQ observed in schizophrenic patients is caused by institutionalization. One way that we investigated the problem was to study patients who were in an institution, but who were not mentally ill. In the 1970s we compared 18 patients with schizophrenia who were receiving long-term care in Shenley Hospital with normal controls and with 10 people receiving long-term care in the Royal Home and Hospital for Incurables in Putney. These latter patients suffered from crippling diseases that did not affect the central nervous system. Most of them had had polio, but one had had arthritis, affecting almost all joints, from childhood, and one had muscular dystrophy (a progressive muscle-wasting disease). A number of cognitive tests were used. The patients with schizophrenia did markedly less well than both other groups, but there were no significant differences between the physically ill patients and the well controls. The mean duration of institutional care of the physically ill was 24 years, and many of them had been invalids at home leading very restricted lives for years before admission to the home in Putney.

These results show that staying in an institution for many years is certainly not sufficient to cause impairments in intelligence. However, in relation to schizophrenia, the question can be more directly addressed by studying patients who would have been in an institution in the 1950s, but are now in the community. One such study, carried out by Kelly and her colleagues in 2000 examined all the patients with schizophrenia (182) in an area of southwest Scotland. At the time only 14% of these patients were in hospital. Nevertheless, the group as a whole showed evidence of impairment on a wide range of tests. For example, on a memory test about 80% of the group showed impaired performance. We have also performed such studies and obtained very similar results. While institutionalization may well have exaggerated the intellectual deficits observed in patients with schizophrenia, it cannot have been the sole cause of these problems. Instead of being placed in large institutions, virtually all patients with schizophrenia are now treated with drugs (see Chapter 4). The drugs used are sometimes referred to as major tranquillizers, and they can have marked side-effects. Patients often report that the drugs make thinking slow and effortful. Given these reports, it is not unreasonable to suggest that drug treatment might cause poor performance on intelligence tests. Somewhat surprisingly, however, there is very little evidence that the drugs have any marked effect on performance on such tests. We conducted a number of studies in which some patients were treated with drugs while others received inert, placebo tablets. We observed very little difference in the test performance of these two groups. There have also been several studies in which intellectual functions were tested at the beginning of the first episode of schizophrenia, before the patients had received any form of treatment. In 1999

Mohamed and his colleagues gave a large number of psychological tests to 94 patients during their first episode of schizophrenia. None of these patients had been treated with drugs for more than two weeks, and 73 of them had never been treated with drugs. All the patients showed impaired performance on nearly all the tests they were given. The average impairment was equivalent to a drop in IQ of 15 points. Very similar results had previously been observed in other studies in which impairments of intellectual function were observed in untreated patients who had been in hospital only for a few days or weeks. These results demonstrate that intellectual impairments cannot be blamed on drug treatment or on institutionalization.

Is there a characteristic pattern of intellectual impairment?

As already noted, the concept of intelligence is based on the observation that people who are good at one kind of test tend also to be good at others. However, at the same time that tests were being developed to measure IQ, neuropsychologists were demonstrating the opposite phenomenon. Circumscribed brain lesions can cause impairment in the performance of one kind of test, while performance on all others remains intact. The French neurologist Paul Broca was the first to demonstrate this in 1861 with his patient known as Tan (real name, Leborgne) who could not speak (except to say, 'tan tan tan'), but could understand speech. This problem was associated with damage to the left inferior frontal region of the brain, which came to be known as Broca's area.

Throughout the 20th century much work was done to develop tests that were sensitive to damage in specific brain regions. Such tests tend to be referred to in terms of the associated brain region, so that a test of the ability to recognize objects from unusual viewpoints might be referred to as a parietal lobe test, while a test of spontaneous verbal fluency – such as 'name all the animals you can

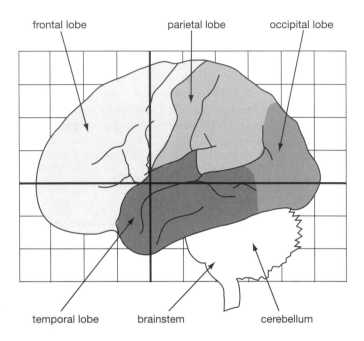

frontal lobe   parietal lobe   occipital lobe

temporal lobe   brainstem   cerebellum

7. The human brain is a lump of tissue weighing almost 1.5 kg and containing about 10 billion neurons (or nerve cells). The brain consists of several large regions, each responsible for different aspects of perceiving, thinking, and acting as well as more basic functions. The brainstem connects the brain to the spinal cord and controls many basic functions such as breathing, eating, and sleeping. The cerebellum is concerned with coordinating skilled movements and maintaining posture and balance. The cerebral cortex, which is divided into left and right hemispheres, is the most highly developed part of the brain. Within each hemisphere there are four lobes. The occipital lobe deals with vision. The parietal lobe is concerned with touch, with sensing the position of the body in space, and with attention. The temporal lobe is involved with hearing and language, with object recognition, and with memory and emotion. The frontal lobe is concerned with performing actions and with decision-making, problem solving, and planning.

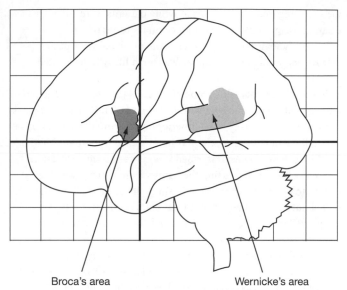

Broca's area   Wernicke's area

8. Paul Broca (1824–80) and Carl Wernicke (1848–1904) studied the effects of brain damage on language. They were the first to show that small regions of the brain have very specific psychological functions. Broca's area lies in the lower part of the frontal cortex on the left. Patients with damage to this region can understand speech, but cannot produce it. Wernicke's area lies in the upper part of the temporal lobe and the lower part of the parietal lobe. Patients with damage to this region can produce speech, but cannot understand it. In the vast majority of people, these areas concerned with language are in the left hemisphere of the brain. When patients with schizophrenia are hallucinating (hearing voices), increased activity is seen in these areas of the brain.

think of' – is referred to as a frontal lobe test. These labels are justified on the basis that patients with parietal lobe lesions tend to do badly on 'unusual views' tasks, while patients with frontal lobe lesions tend to do badly on verbal fluency tasks, though their performance on other tasks remains intact. The reverse logic, that, if someone is impaired on verbal fluency (but not other tasks), then they must have frontal damage, is much more problematic. Nevertheless, before the development of non-invasive techniques for acquiring images of the brain while patients were still alive (see Chapter 5), measuring performance on batteries of neuropsychological tests was one of the principal ways of discovering where brain damage was most likely to be located.

Using this logic, sets of neuropsychological tests have been given to patients with schizophrenia with the aim of identifying those parts of the brain most likely to be functioning abnormally. However, as we shall see in Chapter 5, there is no evidence from brain imaging for the existence of circumscribed lesions in particular locations. Therefore, rather than using the results from neuropsychological testing to talk about damage in brain regions, we shall use them to talk about impaired cognitive functions. We shall refer to tests of executive function, for example, rather than to 'frontal' tests.

It is already clear from our discussion of intelligence that schizophrenic patients tend to perform badly on a whole range of different tests. However, these studies also show that the impairment is much greater on some kinds of task than on others. Routine, well-learned tasks such as reading and mental arithmetic are often unimpaired, while novel tasks that require a flexible approach to problem solving are often severely impaired. There is a striking concordance in the way that different authors have characterized the cognitive areas in which patients with schizophrenia show the greatest impairment – they are memory, attention, and executive function.

The nature of the cognitive impairment associated with schizophrenia

Rather than going into the details on which these conclusions are based, we shall try to indicate what these conclusions tell us about cognitive function in schizophrenia. The interested reader can always go back to the original studies.

One test of executive function on which patients with schizophrenia often perform badly is 'verbal fluency', particularly in the form where the patient has to give all the words she can think of beginning with the letter A (or S, or F). Patients with Alzheimer's disease often perform this task badly as well, but the cause is different. A patient with Alzheimer's disease might no longer know what an apron is, and would not be able to name a picture of an apple. These words are no longer available, and that is why the patient will not produce many words in a verbal fluency test. To use Elizabeth Warrington's term, the patient's store of words has become 'degraded'. But poor performance on this task is also a marker of executive problems. A patient with executive problems knows the words; she knows what an apron is and can name an apple. Her difficulty lies in retrieving the words from the store. Warrington calls this problem 'impaired access'.

So how do we normally find suitable words in a verbal fluency task? We could wait passively for words beginning with A to pop into our head. But we will do much better if we can think of an active strategy for finding the words. We might look around the room for objects beginning with A (amplifier); we might go through categories of objects like fruit to find objects beginning with A (apple); or we might run systematically through the alphabet starting with words beginning AA (aardvark). In these examples, we have thought up for ourselves a strategy for finding words beginning with A and we have then implemented that strategy. Generating and applying a suitable strategy is a typical example of an executive function. The ability to generate and apply strategies is useful for the performance of many different kinds of task. For example, psychologists are very fond of presenting a list of words and then asking patients to repeat back the words a few minutes later. This is a typical memory test. We could just listen passively to the words and hope that we will remember them. We could repeat the words over and over in our heads, but the psychologist will probably prevent this by giving another task to distract us. The best way to remember a list of words is to think about what the words mean. For example, we might make up a sentence for each word. The patient with 'executive problems' fails to use strategies like this when trying to remember a list of words, and as a result her memory for the words is poor. If she is specifically instructed to use a good strategy, her memory improves.

It is clear that problems with executive functions will have a pervasive effect on the performance of a whole range of tasks. For almost any task there will be an optimum strategy that could be adopted, including, of course, the strategy of abandoning the task altogether because enough time has been spent on it or it is too difficult. Tasks that depend least on executive functions are those that have been well practised so that optimum strategy is adopted as a matter of routine. Alternatively, the need for executive functions is minimized if the experimenter tells the subject precisely how the task should be performed and which strategy should be adopted. On tasks like this patients with schizophrenia perform reasonably well.

Is schizophrenia a frontal lobe disorder?

Neuropsychologists believe that executive functions depend upon the prefrontal cortex. Different aspects of executive functioning probably rely upon different regions of prefrontal cortex, although precise relationships are yet to be determined. Once a suitable strategy has been selected by processes acting in the prefrontal cortex, it will be implemented in posterior parts of the brain. For example, the word store that must be accessed in a verbal fluency task is probably located in the left temporal cortex (Wernicke's area; see Figure 8). Thus, the executive processes located in the prefrontal cortex can be seen as being near the top of a hierarchy of control. The executive processes control the function of lower centres located in posterior regions of the brain. Perhaps a loss of executive function is what Kraepelin described as 'dissolution of personality', with a 'loss of mastery over volition, of endeavour, and of ability for independent action'.

In patients with known brain lesions, impairment of executive function is associated with lesions in the frontal lobe, although these often have to be quite large for the impairment to be detected using standard neuropsychological tests. However, these patients are not like people with schizophrenia since they do not typically report hallucinations. On the other hand, as we shall see in Chapter 7, they do sometimes develop delusions, although these do not resemble in content those of patients with schizophrenia.

If executive function depends not only on the prefrontal cortex but also on interactions between the prefrontal cortex and other brain regions, then problems could arise if something went wrong with these interactions. The interactions depend upon long-range connections between brain regions and also on loops involving structures beneath the cortex, such as the basal ganglia. As we shall see in Chapter 7, there is some preliminary evidence for long-range disconnections in the brains of people with schizophrenia.

Test performance and motivation

Any study of schizophrenia is worthless unless there is a certain degree of trust between the patient and the researcher. We need some justification for believing what the patient tells us about his hallucinations and delusions. Likewise we need to have justification for believing that the patient is actually trying to perform the task we have given him. Perhaps he is deliberately performing badly through suspicion of our motives for testing him. Perhaps he simply does not have the motivation to help us by trying to perform well.

These possibilities can never be entirely ruled out, but it is our strong impression that patients we examined were trying to do the various tasks we set them. In Northwick Park Hospital our experimental psychology lab was a small room in the acute psychiatric ward. Patients on the ward had very little to do and frequently knocked on the lab door to ask if there were more tests for them to try. One of our more frightening experiences involved testing a man who had a job of such sensitivity that he would inevitably be suspended from it if there were any hint of a psychotic illness. He was deeply suspicious of us, but determined to perform the psychological tests as well as he possibly could, not realizing that the loss of his job would not be due to intellectual impairment, but to the nature of his bizarre delusions.

It is very difficult to design empirical studies that distinguish between cognitive impairment and lack of motivation, but there have been a few attempts. For example, in 1998 Hellman and his colleagues tried to improve performance on the Wisconsin Card Sorting test (a widely used test of executive function) by giving detailed instructions about how to do the task or by giving rewards of money for good performance. The detailed instructions did improve performance, but the monetary reward had no effect. This result suggests a problem with understanding rather than motivation.

Given these observations, we believe that the poor test performance seen in so many patients with schizophrenia is a true reflection of their abilities. Nevertheless, there is a sense in which the problem is indeed partly one of motivation. As Kraepelin noted, there is a 'loss of mastery over volition'. It is not that the patients don't try to perform the test well, rather they no longer know how to try.

Is the cognitive impairment the same in every patient?

We have suggested that there is evidence for a specific cognitive impairment characteristic of schizophrenia. This evidence comes from looking at the average performance of large numbers of patients across a variety of tests – and for that reason it could be misleading. We know that people with a diagnosis of schizophrenia vary widely both in their performance on psychological tests and in their symptoms. Some patients show marked impairments, while others do not. Some patients might have severe hallucinations and delusions at the time of testing, while others might show only negative features such as poverty of speech and action. Might not these differences affect performance on psychological tests? Hearing abusive voices while you are trying to do a test might very well impair your performance! By looking at the average performance of a large group we may be missing important differences. It is even possible for the average pattern of performance for a group to be different from any individual in that group.

To avoid this problem we studied a series of five patients as single cases. These patients had a diagnosis of schizophrenia and had been ill for many years. All the patients were tested on a very large number of neuropsychological tests and their performance was examined in detail. There was a considerable variation in IQ in this small group, but a common feature of all the patients was poor performance on executive function tasks. Even the patient who had had an IQ of 122 before the onset of illness had difficulty with some of these tests. In this respect the results confirm the conclusions of the group studies – patients with schizophrenia tend to do badly on tests of executive function whether or not their general intellectual performance is impaired.

Is cognitive impairment related to mental state?

The signs and symptoms of schizophrenia vary markedly. This is so whether we are comparing one patient with another or the same patient at different times. This variation in the same patient over time makes it difficult to assign patients to particular subgroups of schizophrenia. Subtypes of schizophrenia have been proposed, and indeed are included in DSM-IV, but attempts to show that these subtypes can be characterized by different intellectual impairments have not been very successful.

In contrast, attempts to define clusters of symptoms, rather than clusters of patients, have led to robust and replicable results. It was Tim Crow who first proposed, on theoretical grounds, that the signs and symptoms of schizophrenia should be categorized as positive or negative – the distinction we have been using to describe the experience of the illness. Positive features are abnormal by their presence and include hallucinations, delusions, incoherent speech, and disorganized behaviour; negative features are abnormal by their absence and include poverty of speech, poverty of action, and blunting of emotions. Subsequently a number of empirical studies have been performed to measure how different signs and symptoms correlate with one another when they are assessed in a cross-section of patients with schizophrenia. These studies have found evidence for three clusters of signs and symptoms rather than the two suggested by Crow. The first cluster, labelled 'reality distortion' by Peter Liddle, consists of delusions and hallucinations. These are the classic symptoms of psychosis, indicating that the patient is out of touch with reality. The second cluster, labelled 'disorganization', includes incoherent speech and inappropriate emotional responses. These are positive features of abnormal thought and behaviour. The third cluster, labelled 'psychomotor poverty', consists of poverty of speech, poverty of action, and blunted emotional responses. These are negative features of abnormal behaviour. These three clusters have been confirmed, with minor variations, in a number of studies.

It is important to remember that these three syndromes relate to clusters of signs and symptoms and not to subgroups of patients. Hallucinations and delusions form a cluster, implying that, if a particular patient reports experiencing hallucinations he or she is likely also to express delusions. However, the presence of hallucinations does not tell us anything about whether or not this patient will show poverty of speech or disorganized behaviour. Some patients may have hallucinations and poverty of speech and disorganized behaviour, while others may only have features from one or two of the syndromes. Our question is whether different kinds of intellectual impairment are associated with these different clusters of signs and symptoms.

The answer is not clear cut, suggesting that the relationship between symptoms and intellectual functioning is not strong. Some studies, mostly involving rather small groups, have not found any relationships. Nevertheless, in the larger studies where relationships have been found there is a considerable degree of consistency. We have already mentioned our study of nearly 300 patients in the Harrow Health District. In this group low IQ scores were associated with poverty of speech (the psychomotor poverty syndrome) and with disorganized speech (the disorganization syndrome). However, there was no relationship between presence of hallucinations and delusions and IQ scores. When performance on the various tests was examined more closely, differences were found in the type of impairment associated with the poverty syndrome and the disorganization syndrome. The errors of patients with poverty of speech and action tended to be of omission. These patients often failed to respond in the time permitted. For example, on a verbal fluency test one patient could name only three animals in three minutes. He commented, 'The only one I can think of is cheetah.' In contrast the errors associated with the disorganization syndrome tend to be of commission, that is patients failed to inhibit inappropriate responses. For example, another patient performing the same verbal fluency task produced the sequence, 'emu, duck, swan, lake, Loch Ness monster, bacon . . . '. In this example, the word 'lake' is closely associated with the word 'swan', but should not have been given since it is not an example of an animal. The word 'bacon' is also inappropriate, and why the patient produced it is difficult to understand, but this inexplicable conjunction of words is typical of the incoherent speech sometimes associated with schizophrenia.

We believe that the relationships found between these syndromes and performance on neuropsychological tests give us a better understanding of some of the features of schizophrenia. These features resemble the impairments of executive function that can be seen in some neurological patients after damage to the frontal cortex and, furthermore, schizophrenic patients with these features show a similar pattern of impairments on neuropsychological

9. Spontaneous drawing by a patient who showed extremely
disorganized behaviour. She was studied by Joze Jensterle and Janez
Mlakar in the University Hospital at Ljubljana. The text in the drawing
combines Slovenian, English, and German words.

tests to that shown by patients with frontal damage. These observations provide clues about the cognitive defects that underlie some aspects of schizophrenia as well as their possible neural basis.

Some researchers have suggested that these problems with executive function represent the core of schizophrenia. These impairments show little change over time and can be found to a greater or lesser degree in all patients. However, there is no immediately obvious relationship between these impairments and the hallucinations and delusions that are still the key features that lead to a diagnosis of schizophrenia. As we have seen, performance on standard neuropsychological tests does not seem to relate to these symptoms. Furthermore, the kind of hallucinations and delusions described by patients with schizophrenia are rarely reported by patients with known brain abnormalities. We shall return to this problem in Chapter 7.

Genius and madness

> Great wits are sure to madness near allied,
> Thin partitions do their bounds divide.
>
> John Dryden, Absalom and Achitophel

We have presented the evidence that people with a diagnosis of schizophrenia tend to perform badly on a whole range of psychological tests, particularly those that require a novel and flexible approach. How is this compatible with the widespread belief that there is a close relationship between madness and genius? The most characteristic feature of the genius, in particular the mad genius, is the novelty of his or her contribution to art or science. Yet the kinds of tests on which patients with schizophrenia do badly are precisely those that require a minimal degree of creativity, like the verbal fluency test. Is it possible that some of their executive problems can actually give rise to creativity? Perhaps a special kind of creativity arises from seeing relationships where the

10. *Self-Portrait, A Meditation*, by Charles Altamont Doyle (1832–93). Doyle painted several strange fantasies and nightmarish scenes, often featuring elves. He exhibited a number of watercolours and pen and ink studies at the Royal Scottish Academy. Doyle illustrated John Bunyan's *Pilgrim's Progress* and produced several illustrations for *London Society* and for humorous books. His interest in the occult was inherited by his son, the author Sir Arthur Conan Doyle. This introspective study was made after epilepsy and alcholism had forced Charles Doyle's incarceration in the Montrose Royal Lunatic Asylum.

rest of us see none or from making the responses that we suppress because we think they are inappropriate.

There are many well-known examples of highly creative people who were also mad – Vincent Van Gogh, Robert Schumann, Friedrich Nietzsche, to name the first that spring to mind. But it is very difficult to know precisely what form the madness took in these figures from the past. In 1987 Nancy Andreasen studied 30 distinguished contemporary writers and their relatives. The writers had a substantially higher rate of mental illness than would have been expected, but these were mainly affective disorders with a predominance of bipolar illnesses, that is alternating periods of elation (mania) and depression. If any illness affecting mood was counted, then 80% of the writers had suffered an attack at some time, but not one of the group had suffered from schizophrenia. Similar results were obtained by Arnold M. Ludwig, who studied around 1,000 people in a whole range of creative professions. These studies could be criticized on the grounds that the creativity of these participants was in the 'normal' range and not at the level of genius. But this criticism cannot be applied to Kay Jamison, who has written about important British and North American writers and artists, including Byron, Tennyson, Melville, William and Henry James, Coleridge, Hemingway, and Virginia Woolf. She also concludes that the madness seen in these and many other highly creative people was manic-depressive psychosis, rather than schizophrenia.

As we have already noted, the distinction between these forms of psychosis remains in some degree arbitrary since independent biological markers are yet to be found. The current consensus is that there is indeed a link between creativity and madness, but the suggestion that the madness in question is manic-depressive psychosis rather than schizophrenia must continue to be treated with caution. In some cases the argument becomes dangerously circular. We have heard it said that the suspicion of schizophrenia in the case of Virginia Woolf (one of her symptoms involved hearing voices) can be dismissed since schizophrenia is so rare in practising authors. Furthermore, there are a few highly creative people who do seem to have suffered from schizophrenia as it is currently defined. The case of John Nash is now well known through the feature film *A Beautiful Mind*. His pioneering developments in economic game theory won him the Nobel Prize, and yet he clearly suffered from paranoid schizophrenia. However, our impression is that his important work was done before the onset of the illness. Another interesting case is that of Richard Dadd, who was probably the most talented English artist of his generation. After a visit to the Holy Land in 1842 he began to suffer from delusions of being persecuted. He described being prompted by voices and became convinced that he was being called upon by divine forces to do battle with the devil, who could assume any shape he desired. In 1843, at the age of 26,

Dadd killed his father, believing that he was killing the devil who had taken his father's shape. He spent the rest of his life in criminal lunatic asylums, first at the Bethlem Hospital and finally at Broadmoor. He continued to paint in prison, producing some of his best work, including *The Fairy Feller's Master Stroke* which is in the permanent collection at the Tate Gallery. This is a technically brilliant piece of work, which is saved from Victorian sentimentality by extreme weirdness. The symptoms of his illness suggest to us a diagnosis of schizophrenia, and it seems unreasonable to dismiss this diagnosis solely on the grounds that he continued to produce good work after the onset of the illness.

> Poetry is the spontaneous overflow of powerful feelings; it takes its origin from emotion recollected in tranquillity
>
> William Wordsworth

A key difference between manic-depressive psychosis and schizophrenia is that the periods of elation and depression are interspersed with periods of normality. Most patients with schizophrenia never return to a normal level of functioning after the first episode. This may be relevant to the apparent lack of creativity in people with schizophrenia. Nancy Andreasen reports that most of the writers she studied wrote when their mood was normal, and not when it was elevated or depressed. This also seems to have been the case for Virginia Woolf. She became completely unproductive in terms of writing when unwell, but she was convinced that the ideas for her books came to her during periods of manic illness. Most people with a diagnosis of schizophrenia never return to a level of normality in which it would be possible to work on any creative ideas revealed through their psychotic experiences. In other words, while it is possible that some of the positive features of schizophrenia might lead to creative ideas, the negative features, the lack of will and the poverty of action which are so often pervasive, are incompatible with the concentrated endeavour required to turn a creative idea into a lasting work of art.

Sketch of an idea for Crazy Jane.
by Richard Dadd. Bethlehem Hospital. London
September 6th 1855.

11. *Sketch of an Idea for Crazy Jane* by Richard Dadd, Bethlehem
Hospital London, 6 September 1855. Richard Dadd (1817–86) was one
of the most talented English painters of his generation. However, in
1843 he murdered his father, believing him to be the devil, and spent the
rest of his life in mental institutions. He continued to paint and
produced some of his best work in these circumstances.

If a schizophrenic illness prevents the manifestation of any creativity associated with psychosis, then we might expect to find more creativity in those people who have mild features of schizophrenia, but never experience an obvious breakdown of function. We would expect to find such people among the relatives of patients with schizophrenia. This idea has received encouragement from a well-known anecdote about the meeting between James Joyce and Carl Jung. Joyce's daughter Lucia was diagnosed with hebephrenic schizophrenia at the age of 25. Two years later, in desperation, Joyce took her to Jung's clinic in Zurich, 'even though Jung had written negatively about Ulysses'. Joyce believed that Lucia was creative like him. Jung concluded that father and daughter were like two people going to the bottom of the sea, 'one falling, one diving'. In other words, Joyce was in control of his unusual ideas and could use them creatively; Lucia's ideas were out of control and could not be used. Lucia spent the rest of her life in and out of various mental hospitals. She died in St Andrew's Hospital in Northampton.

There are also a few empirical studies attempting to show that the relatives of people with schizophrenia are more creative than others. The relationship has been studied most intensively in Iceland, where there are very good records available for identifying the relatives of patients who have been in hospital with psychotic illnesses. In 2001 Karlsson reported that the healthy relatives of these patients excelled over others in authorship of books of fiction or poetry, in general school performance at age 20 years, and in mathematics. These observations applied to schizophrenia as well as affective illnesses. It is interesting to note in this context that one of the best and most informative novels about the experience of schizophrenia, *Angels of the Universe*, is by the Icelandic poet Einar Már Gudmundsson and is based on the life of his schizophrenic brother.

There does seem to be some truth in the romantic idea that there is a relationship between madness and genius. For a very few people, psychotic ideas reflected upon in tranquillity can be the basis of important creative works. But the majority of people with schizophrenia can gain little of value from their psychotic experiences; they have lasting intellectual problems and a high-level 'executive' system that places tragic limits on what they can achieve.

Chapter 4
Schizophrenia and drugs

One of the most exciting scientific developments in the second half of the 20th century concerned the discovery of the role of chemical messengers (called neurotransmitters) in the brain and their importance for understanding how drugs work (see the boxes on neurons, synapses, and neurotransmission below). In parallel with these discoveries, a number of drugs were identified that have a direct effect on many of the symptoms associated with schizophrenia. Some of these drugs can create these symptoms in otherwise healthy people, while others can markedly reduce symptoms in patients who are severely ill. As we have already seen, the latter have had a major impact on the treatment of schizophrenia. Nevertheless, we are still a long way from a cure. The drugs currently available often have unpleasant side-effects, and there are a few patients for whom no suitable pharmacological treatment can be found. By studying the drugs' effects we find clues about the brain mechanisms and neurotransmitters that underlie the symptoms associated with schizophrenia and can thereby discover better forms of treatment.

The neuron

The brain contains about 10 billion neurons (or nerve cells). These neurons are connected together in complex ways and are continuously sending messages to one another. It is this activity in the neurons that enables us to perceive, think, and act. Most neurons consist of three main parts: a central cell body that controls all the activities of the neuron; several branching projections called dendrites that receive messages from other neurons; and an axon, a long fibre that transmits messages to the dendrites of other neurons or to muscles. The messages are transmitted within the neuron from the cell body to the far end of the axon in the form of electrical impulses. Most axons are wrapped in a sheath of myelin (a fatty insulating substance) that increases the efficiency of message transmission.

The synapse

Although axons and dendrites are located extremely close to each other, in most cases the transmission of the message from one neuron to another does not occur through direct contact. Instead, communication between neurons occurs through the release of chemicals into the space between the axon and the dendrites. This space is known as the synapse.

Neurotransmission

The chemical transmission of messages between neurons is known as neurotransmission. When the electrical impulse moves down the axon towards the synapse, this triggers the release of chemicals called neurotransmitters from the axon into the synapse. The neurotransmitters then drift across the synapse and attach themselves to special molecules called receptors in the dendrites of the neighbouring neuron. When a neurotransmitter binds to a receptor in this way, activity in the neighbouring neuron is either stimulated or inhibited. There are many different neurotransmitters and each one can only bind to a specific receptor, rather like a key that only fits into a matching lock. Once it has done its job, the neurotransmitter has to be removed from the synapse. One method is to reabsorb the neurotransmitter back into the axon it came from (known as re-uptake). Transporter molecules in the axon pick up the neurotransmitters from the synapse and carry them back into the cell where they can be used again.

Pink elephants and midget monkeys

Of course, not everyone who is experiencing hallucinations and delusions is suffering from schizophrenia. It is well known that many different kinds of drugs can produce states of intoxication in which hallucinations and delusions occur. These experiences can also occur during withdrawal after prolonged periods of drug taking. One of the best known of these withdrawal states is delirium tremens (often called DTs or the shakes). This occurs when 'drying out' after excessive use of alcohol. People in this state often experience visual hallucinations, the fabled 'pink elephants' of popular imagination.

That's when you start seeing the little animals. You know that stuff about pink elephants? That's bunk. It's *little* animals! Little tiny turkeys in straw hats. Midget monkeys coming through the keyholes. See that guy over there? With him it's beetles. Come the night, he sees beetles crawling all over him. Has to be dark though.

From *The Lost Weekend*, Billy Wilder's 1945
film about an alcoholic

They put a straightjacket on me and tied me to a bed in the sanatorium because I wouldn't stop scratching and hitting myself. Can you imagine what I felt when I saw cockroaches burying their feet into my skin as if into butter? And the rats would bite me with their sharp little teeth. They were all over my body, but I was most distressed by the ones on my face, which I couldn't see but could feel. I yelled for help over and over.

From *Delirium Tremens*, a novel by Ignacio Solares

Similar states can also arise during withdrawal after excessive use of sedatives – barbiturates like Nembutal or tranquillizers such as Valium. These states are very different from those associated with schizophrenia. During withdrawal from drugs, patients are disoriented and agitated. Furthermore, the hallucinations and delusions they experience are not sustained, but constantly changing and usually short-lived.

Hallucinogenic drugs

As their name implies, hallucinogenic drugs can also cause the user to experience hallucinations. These drugs are taken precisely because they produce changes in perception and thinking, experiences that were an important part of many ancient and some modern cultures. 'This is how one ought to see, how things really are', said Aldous Huxley in *The Doors of Perception*, describing the effects of mescaline. The effects of these drugs are immediate and are not associated with disorientation or agitation, so that the experience is more similar to schizophrenia than delirium. The most widely used hallucinogenic drugs are psilocybin (magic mushroom) and mescaline, which are naturally occurring plant substances, and lysergic acid methylamide (LSD) and MDMA (3–4 methylenedioxymethamphetamine, ecstasy), which are synthetic drugs.

All these drugs produce remarkable mental changes, but while the experiences are very vivid, they are not like those associated with schizophrenia. Delusions are rare and perceptual changes are more common than full-blown hallucinations. Sometimes perception is heightened, as seems to have been the case for Aldous Huxley on mescaline.

> I looked down by chance, and went on passionately staring by choice, at my own crossed legs. Those folds in the trousers – what a labyrinth of endlessly significant complexity! And the texture of the grey flannel – how rich, how deeply mysteriously sumptuous!

Sometimes perception is distorted, leading to illusions in various sensory modalities. Such an illusion was described by Albert Hoffman, the chemist who discovered the hallucinogenic properties of LSD in 1943.

> The lady next door, whom I scarcely recognised, brought me milk – She was no longer Mrs R, but rather a malevolent, insidious witch with a coloured mask.

Frequently the hallucinations consist of shifting and changing patterns superimposed on the subject's visual field.

> I – noticed that the various creases and ripples in my blanket were moving all over its surface, as if snakes were crawling around underneath it.
>
> Description of the effects of LSD from the
> Erowid Experience Vaults

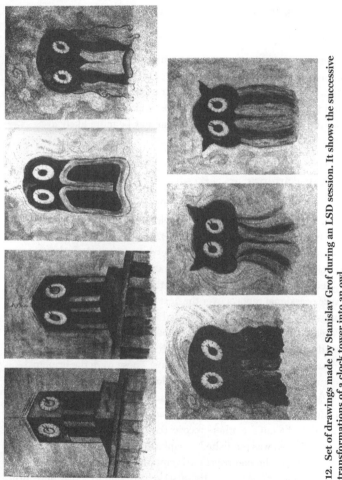

12. Set of drawings made by Stanislav Grof during an LSD session. It shows the successive transformations of a clock tower into an owl.

Aldous Huxley saw constantly changing coloured patterns when he closed his eyes.

> The field of vision was filled with brightly coloured, constantly changing structures that seemed to be made of plastic or enamelled tin.

There are accounts of episodes of schizophrenia occurring after taking LSD, but such cases are not common. Furthermore, the direction of the causal link between developing schizophrenia and taking LSD is not known. It is possible that people who are predisposed to develop schizophrenia may be more likely to try LSD.

Amphetamines

The association of schizophrenia with amphetamine (speed) and similar drugs is much stronger. The immediate effects of these drugs are not at all like those of schizophrenia: users become excited, euphoric, and tireless. However, an association between a psychosis resembling schizophrenia and amphetamine use was first noted in 1938, only three years after the drug was introduced. There were occasional reports over the next 20 years of similar isolated cases, but in 1958 Connell published an account of 42 people who developed schizophrenia-like psychoses while taking amphetamine. He described psychotic illnesses with delusions accompanied, in some cases, by auditory hallucinations. These were the principal features of the disorder, and Connell noted that disorientation was unusual. The disorder was very like schizophrenia, but differed in its duration. Three-quarters of the cases recovered within a week, and almost all of the others recovered within a month. A similar series of cases was published in Japan. Tatetsu studied almost 500 patients who had psychiatric complications following methamphetamine use. Of these, 92% were said to show some form of psychiatric disorder. In most cases this was of a mild nature, but 19% of the sample showed a schizophrenia-like psychosis. Tatetsu also described a rapid improvement after the drug was stopped, but this was not as frequent as it was in Connell's series, and many did not make a full recovery.

After the publication of these two series of cases of amphetamine psychosis, many more cases were reported and it became evident that schizophrenia-like psychoses occurred in association with the use of other stimulant drugs including cocaine, phenmetrazine, methylphenidate (Ritalin), and ephedrine. These reports clearly demonstrated that the use of amphetamine is associated with the development of psychotic symptoms resembling those associated with schizophrenia. But can we conclude that amphetamine use directly causes these experiences? Does everyone develop psychotic symptoms after taking amphetamine? Perhaps the symptoms only occurred in individuals already predisposed to develop schizophrenia. Or it might be the case that individuals who were predisposed to schizophrenia were particularly likely to take amphetamine (as has been suggested for the rare cases of psychosis associated with taking LSD). These questions can only be answered by giving amphetamine to volunteers in controlled laboratory conditions. Such experiments were conducted 30 years ago. It is doubtful if it would be possible to conduct them today.

Griffiths and his colleagues gave 10 mg of amphetamine hourly to four volunteers who, all in all, had about 50 mg of the drug each day. After between one and five days, all four became paranoid and developed delusions of reference (believing, for example, that television or radio broadcasts were about them, or that others were talking or thinking about them). Fortunately, recovery was rapid in all cases. Angrist and Gershon gave higher total doses of amphetamines (over a period of up to 75 hours) to four volunteers. Two of these developed clear-cut psychotic symptoms, while the others described what we would probably now call partial symptoms. The experiences of these volunteers were recorded in some detail. There are clear accounts of paranoid delusions, olfactory hallucinations, and auditory hallucinations in which

Responses of subject A to amphetamine over 28.75 hours

Observations at approximately two-hourly intervals:

1. 'The other patients went to bed and the atmosphere changed. I was the centre of attention. I didn't want to talk because I was afraid I'd say something and the nurses would make a report and you'd cut me off. I felt the nurse behind me and felt like I had to hide or something.'

2. During the night one patient awoke, came into the day-room and spoke of 'brainwashing'. 'It seemed she thought I was doing it to her, making her sicker with my mind. Then I thought there was another person involved – putting thoughts into both our minds or using my mind to cure her.' Asked if he believed in telepathy, he answered: 'When I'm stoned I do because it feels so real.'

3. He then began to feel more relaxed but still worried about the nurses' observations and thought others could notice his body odour.

4. He thought discussions between other patients and the investigator concerned him and was afraid to get up from a table for fear that they could tell he was high and would watch him.

5. After lunch he was told to lie down by an aide. He didn't want to but did so 'to avoid an argument'. Lying down he 'felt sure' that the investigator had 'sneakily' cut his medication by substituting placebo tablets and that the amphetamine was being excreted in his perspiration, causing a strong body odour that he actually smelled.

6. At this time he heard the voices of other patients in the ward discussing him in the third person: 'He's stupid.', 'Why's he doing it.', 'He's not doing anything.', 'He's just staying up.'

7. He was afraid to leave the ward for a taped interview because 'other people look at you and seem to know'. He also smelled faeces and thought he had been incontinent but checked and found none.

8. Taking his temperature in the bathroom he noticed someone in a lab across the street and felt that he had been 'planted' there to watch him.

9. Four hours after amphetamine was cut he still felt that other patients on the ward were watching him; this subsided after three additional hours.

10. He also noticed that the odour he attributed to the amphetamine in his perspiration intensified whenever he was in close proximity to the nursing staff, that is when pulse and blood pressure were taken.

The effects of amphetamine on neurotransmission

Most drugs work by interfering with neurotransmission in the brain. This interference can happen in many ways. Drugs that cause receptors to be over-stimulated are called agonists. Those that prevent receptors from being stimulated are called antagonists. Amphetamine is a drug with special relevance for schizophrenia since in large doses it can cause hallucinations and delusions. It is a dopamine agonist – it stimulates the axons of neurons containing dopamine, causing the synapse to be flooded with this neurotransmitter. This causes over-stimulation of the dopamine receptors (there are five different types) in the adjacent neuron. For reasons still unknown, over-stimulation of the dopamine system causes people to experience delusions and hallucinations.

voices are heard discussing the patient in the third person, one of Schneider's first-rank symptoms of schizophrenia.

This work is generally held to show that if sufficient amphetamine is given, psychosis will be produced. It has long been established that amphetamines and related drugs act by producing a functional excess of the neurotransmitters dopamine and noradrenaline. Animal experiments have shown that their effects in producing psychotic symptoms relate to dopamine rather than to noradrenaline.

Cannabis

Cannabis, the active component of marijuana, is one of a number of other drugs associated with the development of psychosis. But in the case of cannabis the nature of this association has caused some controversy. Acute psychotic reactions to cannabis have long been known to occur. Indeed, the diagnosis of 'cannabis psychosis' was widely made at one time. The thinking behind this proposal, at least in some cases, was coloured by the idea that a cannabis psychosis might be less serious and the outlook less pessimistic than would be the case with a 'true' schizophrenic illness. There is now a good deal of evidence against this optimistic view. The use of cannabis among schizophrenic patients is associated with greater severity of psychotic symptoms and earlier and more frequent relapses.

The use of cannabis is now thought to be an independent risk factor in the development of schizophrenia. The strongest evidence for this comes from a study of Swedish conscripts who were followed up for a 15-year period after they entered the army. Men who were heavy cannabis users at the time of conscription were six times more likely to develop schizophrenia than non-users. Furthermore, it has been reported that cannabis-using relatives of schizophrenic patients themselves have an increased risk of schizophrenia. In relation to our own work, we have recently found in the Edinburgh

High Risk Study that in genetically predisposed individuals high cannabis use is associated with the development of psychotic symptoms. This suggests that there is an interaction between genetic and environmental factors. An environmental effect (cannabis use) increases the likelihood of developing schizophrenia in individuals who are already at genetic risk (relatives of patients with schizophrenia).

Recently, the mechanisms through which cannabis exerts its effect on the brain have been identified, and these findings may eventually help us to understand why cannabis use can sometimes lead to psychotic symptoms. Specific sites have been found in the brain where cannabis takes effect. At these sites, cannabis binds to specific receptors on neurons (the cannabinoid receptors). As a result of this work it has been possible to study the precise role of the cannabinoid receptors in animals. They have been shown to be involved in responses to pain and reward, and in aspects of movement. It has also been possible to develop a special strain of mouse in which a receptor gene has been disrupted or 'knocked out'. These receptor knock-out mice are said to exhibit behavioural alterations which may parallel cannabis intoxication and some features of schizophrenia. This is all rather speculative, since animal models of schizophrenia can never be entirely satisfactory – it is simply not possible to demonstrate delusions and hallucinations, the key features of schizophrenia, in mice and rats. Nevertheless, these new discoveries suggest potential mechanisms that can at least be considered as possible explanations for the association between cannabis use and the development of schizophrenia.

Angel dust, special K, and ecstasy

Phencyclidine (PCP or angel dust) was developed as a general anaesthetic in the late 1950s. Early on in its use, it was noted that up to half of the patients anaesthetized with this drug developed paranoid symptoms and hallucinations that persisted for up to

72 hours afterwards. Similar effects could even be produced with small doses that were not enough to reduce the level of consciousness. Perceptual alterations occurred in association with impairments in problem solving. The drug was taken out of clinical use in 1965, but in the 1960s and 1970s its misuse was quite common. Low-dose intoxication is reported to induce excitement but also agitation, hallucinations, delusions, paranoia, incoherence of thought, and some catatonic features. It was reported that when phencyclidine was given to schizophrenic patients, thought disorder, disturbances of body image, and inappropriate emotional responses became worse.

Although some psychotic states produced by phencyclidine intoxication were similar to those seen in schizophrenia, there were also many reports of confusion and disorientation. Phencyclidine has its major effect at receptors for glutamine (an amino acid, or protein building-block, involved in neurotransmission), and this mechanism of action underlies the PCP/NMDA theory of schizophrenia put forward in the 1990s (NMDA stands for N-methyl-D-aspartic acid, another type of amino acid). The drug also, however, has effects on a number of other neurotransmitters, including acetylcholine, serotonin, and probably dopamine.

Also of relevance are the effects of ketamine. This is another anaesthetic, structurally related to phencyclidine. It was developed in the 1960s and although it is not in medical use, it is still in use in veterinary practice. In human subjects it produces euphoria, out-of-body experiences, and, at high doses, psychotic features, including hallucinations and delusions. Although not a particularly common drug of abuse, it was a part of the drug scene in the 1970s, when it was referred to as 'special K'. It is an NMDA receptor antagonist. More widely used in the 1990s, and indeed still at the present time, is ecstasy or MDMA (methylene-dioxy-methamphetamine). This is a serotonin and dopamine agonist and is said to produce increased empathy and emotional expressiveness. These feelings give way to disinhibition, euphoria, perceptual distortions, and hallucinations at high doses. As has been widely reported in the popular press, its use on the drug and dance scene has been associated with occasional deaths.

Antipsychotic drugs

The precise mechanisms by which drugs produce psychotic states are not yet known. It is already clear, however, that it is the drugs that stimulate the dopamine system, dopamine agonists like amphetamine, that produce psychotic states most similar to schizophrenia. This whole issue was made much more interesting by the discovery that drugs that successfully treat schizophrenic symptoms act by blocking dopamine receptors in the brain.

In 1950, chlorpromazine was synthesized in France. This drug was found to have very powerful sedative properties, producing a state of 'artificial hibernation', in which patients remained conscious but showed marked indifference to their surroundings (and hypothermia). The drug was first used in conjunction with anaesthesia, but the surgeon Laborit suggested to his psychiatric colleagues that chlorpromazine might be helpful with psychotic patients. His suggestion was taken up by Delay and Deniker, who introduced chlorpromazine into psychiatric practice in 1952. On the basis of clinical observation, they considered that this drug was not acting in these patients simply as a super sedative, but was directly affecting psychotic symptoms. This idea was not initially widely accepted. By the late 1950s, however, large-scale trials in the United States showed that sedatives (barbiturates) were no better than placebo in relieving schizophrenic symptoms, whereas chlorpromazine, and other drugs in its class (the phenothiazines), were consistently effective.

There is now no doubt that chlorpromazine and similar drugs are effective in relieving the delusions, hallucinations, and disorganization of thinking characteristic of acute episodes of schizophrenia. In a review covering the first two decades of the use of these drugs, Davis and Garver found that 86% of controlled studies showed chlorpromazine to be superior to placebo, and they also noted that in all 26 trials in which more than 500 mg per day of chlorpromazine was given the drug definitely had greater effect than placebo. The discovery of a new class of drugs that relieved the fundamental symptoms of schizophrenia represented an enormous advance.

In the early 1960s, Paul Janssen and his colleagues derived a new group of drugs, the butyrophenones, which were also effective in treating psychotic symptoms. These drugs, along with many others, were tested on animals. Two of the animal tests used turned out to predict very well which drugs would have antipsychotic properties. When laboratory animals are given amphetamine, they become over-active and make repetitive movements. Antipsychotic drugs block these effects of amphetamine. When animals are given apomorphine (a drug derived from the opiate morphine), they also become over-active and tend to vomit. Antipsychotic drugs block these effects too. Both amphetamine and apomorphine act by

The effects of antipsychotic drugs

Although there are many different kinds of antipsychotic drug, they all have the same property of blocking dopamine receptors. Antipsychotic drugs fit into (or bind with) dopamine receptors without stimulating them. Thus they prevent the receptors from being stimulated by dopamine. By reducing stimulation of the dopamine system, antipsychotic drugs eliminate the hallucinations and delusions experienced by someone who has taken large amounts of amphetamine. These drugs also reduce the severity of hallucinations and delusions in most people suffering from schizophrenia.

stimulating the dopamine system in the brain, so these observations suggested that the effects of the new antipsychotic drugs were related to their ability to reduce activity in the dopamine system.

Other clues came from studies of patients. Clinicians observed that, while antipsychotics relieved schizophrenic symptoms, they also produced movement disorders, stiffness and slowness, resembling problems associated with Parkinson's disease. By this time it was known, on the basis of the work of Hornykiewicz, that dopamine was greatly reduced in the brains of patients who had died with Parkinson's disease. Thus, the symptoms of Parkinson's disease seemed to be due to a failure of the dopamine system. In 1963 Carlsson and Lindquist proposed that phenothiazines like chlorpromazine might act specifically by blocking dopamine

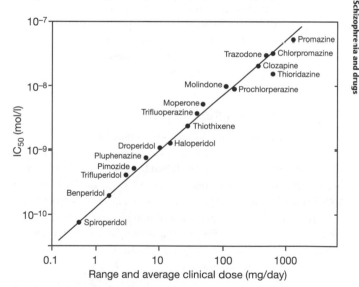

13. **The clinical efficacy of antipsychotic drugs depends on their ability to block dopamine receptors. The smaller the concentration of drug that inhibits the release of dopamine by 50% (IC_{50}), the smaller the effective clinical dose. Figure from Seeman et al. (1976).**

receptors in the brain. Arvid Carlsson over many years carried out a series of experiments on the role of dopamine in the brain, and in 2000 was awarded the Nobel Prize for this work.

On the basis of the psychosis-inducing properties of the dopamine agonist amphetamine and the fact that antipsychotic drugs block dopaminergic transmission, the 'dopamine hypothesis', that is the hypothesis that some schizophrenic symptoms are due to an excess of dopamine in the brain, was put forward. This hypothesis was very extensively investigated throughout the 1970s and a good deal of evidence was found (albeit circumstantial) to support it. It was discovered that there are at least five kinds of dopamine receptor. The clinical efficacy of antipsychotic drugs in treating schizophrenic symptoms is directly related to their ability to block just one of these, known as the D_2 receptor. Throughout the 1970s and early 1980s the view that D_2 receptor blockade was the essential feature for antipsychotic action prevailed, and the pharmaceutical companies directed their efforts to producing more and more pure blockers of D_2 receptors. However, these efforts failed to produce a drug with greater antipsychotic effects.

Atypical antipsychotics

In 1988 John Kane and his colleagues published a study of clozapine. This drug is a relatively weak D_2 blocker, but has wide-ranging pharmacological effects. It had been introduced many years before, but had been taken out of use in many parts of the world in 1976 because it sometimes has serious side-effects on white blood cells. Kane and his colleagues showed that clozapine had significantly greater benefits in terms of antipsychotic effects than chlorpromazine when given to patients with schizophrenia whose symptoms had been difficult to treat.

A major problem with the use of antipsychotic drugs is their unpleasant side-effects, resembling the disorders of movement and thinking associated with Parkinson's disease. Clozapine seems to produce fewer such side-effects, while having at least as much effect on psychotic symptoms as older antipsychotics like chlorpromazine. This observation suggests that movement side-effects are not an inevitable consequence of antipsychotic action and raises the possibility of finding new drugs that are potent antipsychotics but have few or no side-effects. Since the precise mechanism of action of antipsychotics remains a mystery, one strategy is to study drugs that are similar to clozapine.

Clozapine is a drug with complex pharmacology. Which, if any, of the known mechanisms of action of this drug is relevant to its effect in treatment-resistant schizophrenic patients is not known. Nonetheless, following its introduction pharmaceutical companies put much effort into developing drugs that shared clozapine's property of blocking D_2 receptors and also of blocking serotonin (5-HT_{2A}) receptors. These drugs are referred to as 'atypical' antipsychotics. In general, this means that they, like clozapine, have an antipsychotic effect without severe side-effects. There is no evidence, however, that any of the new 'atypicals' are any better than clozapine in the treatment of schizophrenia.

Kapur and Remington have suggested that the antipsychotic action of clozapine and the other 'atypical' antipsychotics does not involve serotonin or other neurotransmitters, but only the dopamine system and D_2 receptors in particular. They propose that the unusual effects of these drugs result from 'fast dissociation' from the D_2 receptor. This means that the antipsychotic effect can occur without obvious motor side-effects. In other words, according to Kapur and Remington, all antipsychotics block dopamine D_2 receptors but some dissociate from these receptors more quickly than others. The quicker the dissociation, the fewer the motor side-effects will be. Action on other neurotransmitter systems is neither necessary nor sufficient. This proposal is a revival of the dopamine hypothesis of antipsychotic drug action and, if correct, provides a way forward for increasing our understanding of drug treatment and for producing better drugs.

Dopamine and schizophrenia

Although the value of antipsychotic drugs in treating delusions and hallucinations is established beyond doubt, as is their efficacy when used as a maintenance treatment in preventing relapse, all of this evidence concerns positive symptoms. We do not have similar clues relating neurotransmission to negative, or deficit, symptoms. Yet it is these symptoms that may be the more disabling, as so clearly described by the young man we quoted at the beginning of Chapter 1.

While successful treatment of positive symptoms seems to depend on blocking dopamine receptors, there is still no direct evidence that schizophrenic symptoms are due to an excess of brain dopamine. Extensive experimental work has failed to provide evidence of increased dopamine turnover in the brains of people with schizophrenia. Postmortem brain studies have revealed increases in the densities of dopamine D_2 receptors in the brains of people who had had schizophrenia during life, but it is not clear whether this is due to the illness or was caused by treatment with antipsychotic drugs. This question can only be answered by examining the brains of patients who have never been treated with antipsychotics. As a result the issue will probably never be resolved. The value of antipsychotic drugs in the treatment of schizophrenia is so well established that it would be considered unethical not to treat patients with schizophrenia with these drugs. Of course, there are areas of the world where people with schizophrenia do not have the benefit of drug treatment, but in these areas there are no facilities for carrying out the kind of postmortem studies required.

However, dopamine receptors can be assessed while patients are still alive using positron emission tomography (PET), a scanning technique that uses radioactive substances to produce three-dimensional images showing chemical activity in tissues. Such work is currently being conducted in the United States and in Europe, but the results are somewhat conflicting. Some studies have found evidence of excessive D_2 receptors in schizophrenia, others have found no differences between patients and controls. It is probably fair to conclude that there is something wrong with the dopamine system in schizophrenia, but this cannot yet be pinned down more precisely to an abnormality in the D_2 receptor.

The striking ability of certain drugs to create or suppress psychotic hallucinations and delusions is clear evidence that these experiences can be caused by changes in brain function. We seem tantalizingly close to discovering the nature of these changes, but so far the details have eluded us.

Chapter 5
Biological factors

Ever since schizophrenia was first defined much research has been devoted to discovering its cause. Some have believed that there must be a biological basis for the disorder, while others have believed equally strongly in social or psychological causes. The proponents of these two views have tended to have little common ground. In the hundred-year search for the cause of schizophrenia, both the biologists and the sociologists have, at times, had the upper hand. In recent years, however, the emphasis has certainly been upon biological causes.

Kraepelin considered that he was defining a disorder that would in time be shown to have a specific pathology in the brain. In order to discover this pathology he collaborated with the neuropathologist Alois Alzheimer, who first discovered the characteristic brain pathology associated with the form of dementia now known as Alzheimer's disease.

Kraepelin quoted the work of Alzheimer in his book on dementia praecox and wrote,

> the morbid anatomy of dementia praecox does not show microscopically any striking changes of the cranial contents, . . . on the other hand it has been shown that in the cortex we have . . . severe and widespread disease of the nerve tissue. Alzheimer has

described deep-spreading changes in the cortical cells, especially in the deep layers, the nuclei are very much swollen, the nuclear membrane greatly wrinkled, the body of the cell considerably shrunk with a tendency to degeneration.

Kraepelin thought that these observations showed that the pathological processes associated with schizophrenia affected only the most highly developed (recently evolved) parts of the brain. However, Alzheimer's observations have not been confirmed in subsequent studies. To quote a recent review, 'Despite a hundred years' research, the neuropathology of schizophrenia remains obscure'.

Sir Thomas Clouston was a psychiatrist working in Edinburgh at about the same time as Kraepelin. Although very well known locally in his day, his work on schizophrenia, which was extensive, has not stood the test of time. Sir Thomas's system of classification was one that he devised himself, and he considered that his concept of adolescent insanity was a part of Kraepelin's concept of dementia praecox. He carried out experiments in which he investigated the structure of the palate in patients with adolescent insanity and those with other conditions (see Figure 14), but these observations have never been confirmed.

Familial and genetic factors

Both Kraepelin and Clouston considered that hereditary factors were important in the aetiology of schizophrenia, and the first study of the familial occurrence of schizophrenia was undertaken by Rudin in Kraepelin's department. The matter has been continuously investigated ever since. By pooling data from a large number of studies carried out in Europe between 1920 and 1987, Irving Gottesman was able to show that the risk of schizophrenia increases from approximately 1% in the general population to 50% in the offspring of two schizophrenic patients and in identical twins

1. Typical

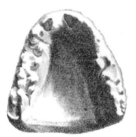

2. Neurotic

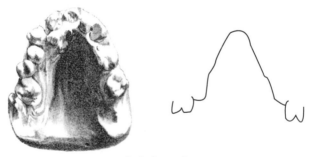

3. Deformed

14. Clouston's data show a clear relationship between a 'deformed' palate and adolescent insanity (schizophrenia), but no one has ever followed up this finding.

The class of persons	typical palate	neurotic palate	deformed palate
General population	40.5% (245)	40.5% (245)	19% (115)
Adolescent insanity	12% (21)	33% (56)	55% (94)

of schizophrenics. In other words, if both of your parents have schizophrenia or you have an identical twin with schizophrenia, then there is a 50% chance that you will also receive the diagnosis at some point. These findings are strongly suggestive of a hereditary factor in schizophrenia. However, families share environments as well as genes. In the past, tuberculosis, caused by an infectious agent, and rickets, caused by vitamin deficiency resulting from poor diet and lack of sunlight, were both highly familial. Gottesman himself pointed out that juvenile delinquency and adult criminality show familial clustering very similar to that shown in relation to schizophrenia.

Two main methods have been employed for disentangling the effects of shared genes from the effects of shared environment. One of these is to look at pairs of twins. Monozygotic (identical) twins have exactly the same genes, but dizygotic twins are no more similar genetically than other brothers and sisters; thus the two types of twins differ substantially in genetic terms but generally speaking they are very similar in environmental terms. Comparison of the concordance rates (shared susceptibility) between monozygotic and dizygotic twins is, therefore, likely to clarify the issue of whether the familial tendency is due to shared genetic material or to shared environment. Such comparisons have been made for schizophrenia, and it is always the case that monozygotic twins show a substantially higher concordance rate.

The second method is to look at children who have a schizophrenic parent but who have been adopted at birth. Such studies are not easy, but several have been conducted. These investigations showed that children adopted away from their biological parents at birth were at significantly greater risk of later developing schizophrenia if there was schizophrenia among their biological relatives, but not if it was present among their adoptive relatives. These findings demonstrate that the enhanced tendency to develop schizophrenia in these people was not due to a shared environment but to shared genetic material.

The twin and adoption studies provide good evidence that genetic factors play a major role in the development of schizophrenia, but equally it is clear that this role is not absolute. The concordance between monozygotic twins is of the order of 50% (contrasting with the 10% of dizygotic twins) but, of course, the genetic material of these individuals is identical. If this were a purely genetic condition, concordance would be 100%. Furthermore, looking at large samples of schizophrenic patients it is very clear that by no means all have a family history of the condition. This was certainly the case in large studies we have conducted. In the study of all schizophrenic patients discharged from hospitals in Harrow between 1975 and 1985, all relevant case notes were scrutinized for information on family history. A family tree was drawn up for each patient in consultation with that patient and a relative. In more than 70% of these cases no family history could be found, and this applied not just to schizophrenia but to psychotic illness generally. Similarly, in his review Gottesman noted that 89% of patients have parents who are not schizophrenic, 81% have no affected first-degree relatives, and 63% show no family history of the disorder whatsoever. Nonetheless, the fact that genetic factors clearly play a role in the development of schizophrenia is an important clue to the cause of the condition.

When we look for mental illness in the family of a patient, we have to depend upon what the relatives tell us. There is always a possibility that this information may not be accurate. The consistency of figures such as those provided by Gottesman would suggest that there are no huge discrepancies, but sometimes families are out of touch with their relatives and it is not possible to get an accurate account. This problem frequently occurs with patients who are seriously ill, since a severe mental illness can cause a breakdown in family relationships. Sometimes, for reasons related to stigma, family history is concealed from doctors, and indeed we have come across cases where the family history is concealed from some family members. In one example, the paternal grandmother of a patient revealed that, although she had claimed to be a widow for nearly 40 years, she did, in fact, visit her husband in a mental hospital every month. While her son knew his father to be alive and to be suffering from schizophrenia, his wife believed that her father-in-law had died before the Second World War and she had no knowledge that he had ever been mentally ill. She, therefore, innocently but falsely reported that there was no history of mental illness in the family. We have no means of knowing how often this sort of thing occurs, but even if it is more widespread than we might think, it is clear from concordance rates of 50% in identical twins that genetics is not the sole answer to the cause of schizophrenia.

Since modern methods of genetic research were developed, these have been applied with enthusiasm to the study of psychiatric disorders. Researchers were encouraged by the great successes achieved using RFLP (restriction fragment length polymorphisms) linkage methods. Using these methods, the faulty gene has been identified in several hereditary disorders such as Huntington's disease, Duchenne's muscular dystrophy, and cystic fibrosis. However, these disorders have a simple form of inheritance in which predictable numbers of each new generation are affected by the disorder according to a clear pattern. With schizophrenia the situation is rarely so straightforward. The pattern of inheritance is complex or irregular. Familial clustering in schizophrenia could be due to a single gene, to a few genes, or to many genes, or indeed to all three different mechanisms operating in different families. So far the evidence from genetic studies suggests that there may be several genes, each with a rather small effect. These genes interact with one another and with environmental factors to influence the susceptibility of a person to schizophrenia. However, none of these genes are either necessary or sufficient to cause schizophrenia.

Most laboratory studies involve comparing genetic material from people in the same family who do or do not suffer from schizophrenia. Another method involves studying conditions associated with a known genetic abnormality which seems to increase the incidence of schizophrenia. One such abnormality is velo-cardio facial syndrome. People with this condition have distinctive facial abnormalities (including cleft palate), learning disability, and heart problems. The condition is caused by the deletion of a small segment of the long arm of chromosome 22 (referred to as 22q11.2 deletion). There is an unusually high rate of psychotic illness in people with this velo-cardio facial syndrome. By studying these people we may discover clues to the genetic basis of schizophrenia. Nevertheless, even if it can be shown how deletions of chromosome 22 are relevant to the development of psychotic illness in people with velo-cardio facial syndrome, this can account for only a very small proportion of patients with schizophrenia.

The main purpose of the genetic studies of schizophrenia is to try to identify a genetic abnormality underlying schizophrenia. Once a responsible gene has been detected, then the normal function of that gene can be elucidated. This would provide an important clue as to what might be going wrong in schizophrenia. If such a discovery could be made, it is probable that it could lead to the development of rational treatments that might be more successful than those that have been employed so far. Such a discovery could revolutionize the treatment and management of patients with schizophrenia. Given this possibility, it is not surprising that a great amount of effort has gone into genetic studies of schizophrenia, but so far the results have been disappointing. The very great difficulty for genetic studies of schizophrenia is that there is no objective marker for the disorder, and there is no clear pattern of inheritance. In the disorders for which genetic advances have been successful, such as Huntington's disease, the pattern of inheritance is well known. In some cases, for example with cystic fibrosis, it is possible to separate the ill from the well family members at a very early stage because the biochemistry of the condition is understood and a biochemical marker for the diagnosis exists. The situation in schizophrenia is very different. Much work, therefore, continues to be devoted to discovering biological markers.

Searching for biological markers

Many different types of biological investigation have been undertaken in seeking the cause of schizophrenia. Extensive investigations were carried out throughout the 20th century. Whenever a new measurement or technique was developed, this was applied to the problem of schizophrenia. In most cases there was no theoretical basis for making these investigations – it was simply a matter of trying the new technique with schizophrenic patients in the hope that something interesting would emerge. Nitrogen metabolism was investigated, the possibility that there could be some general circulatory problem was considered, the body build of patients was studied, and there were extensive investigations of hormones. In the 1960s, considerable interest was generated by the 'pink spot' phenomenon, whereby a substance identified as 3,4-dimethyloxyphenylethylamine (DMPE) was found in the urine of patients with schizophrenia. This was thought to be evidence of abnormal metabolism of a specific group of chemicals, including dopamine, in schizophrenic patients. The results could not, in the end, be replicated, and it was clear that there were many possible sources of the finding.

Abnormalities of brain structure

A more fruitful approach has concerned neuropathological studies of the brain after death and, more recently, neuro-imaging investigations of the brain in life. As mentioned above, Kraepelin encouraged neuropathological investigations of the brains of patients with schizophrenia at around the turn of the 19th century. Extensive work was carried out by Alzheimer and by Wernicke. These researchers described many pathological changes. They spoke of atrophy (wasting away) of neurons, areas where the myelin insulating sheath of neurons had broken down, and abnormalities they described as 'metachromatic bodies'. This work was carried out at a time when techniques for preserving and visualizing brain tissue were in their infancy, and the importance of controlled investigations was not recognized. In 1924 Dunlap did a 'blind' comparison of the brains of eight patients with schizophrenia and five controls. He arranged for these brains to be examined by three independent observers who did not know which brains came from the patient group and which from the control group. The observers carried out cell counts in the areas where abnormalities had been described, and they found no differences between patients and controls. This careful study cast a good deal of doubt upon earlier work, and neuropathological studies became much less extensive.

Investigation of the nervous system during life was not possible until 1919, when pneumoencephalography was introduced by the neurosurgeon Dandy. This technique involves removing some of cerebrospinal fluid from the spaces around the spinal cord and replacing it with air. The air rises up the spinal canal until it outlines the cerebral ventricles (the four natural cavities within the brain that are normally filled with cerebrospinal fluid, see Figure 15), so that these appear black on an X-ray picture. This technique was first applied to patients with schizophrenia in 1927 by Jacobi and Winkler, who claimed that 18 of 19 schizophrenic patients showed enlargement of the cerebral ventricles. A number of other early studies were carried out and most reached similar conclusions, although few used control subjects. Pneumoencephalography is an unpleasant procedure for the subject – it is usually associated with headache and vomiting, and just occasionally the changes in pressure inside the skull can have serious and even fatal consequences. Because of this, in 1929, the American radiological authorities declared that it was unethical to use normal controls in pneumoencephalographic investigations. This placed considerable limitations on subsequent studies, although some were carried out in Japan and in some other countries, and these also tend to support Jacobi and Winkler's work.

In 1973 Hounsfield introduced the technique of computerized

transverse axial scanning (usually called CT scanning). At that time, this was a complex procedure that could take over an hour. Today, it takes only a couple of minutes. Even when it was introduced, however, it had the great advantage of being relatively safe and free of unpleasant side-effects, so that it could quite legitimately be carried out on control subjects. In 1976 we reported that patients with chronic schizophrenia had larger cerebral ventricles than normal controls, and this finding has been replicated many times.

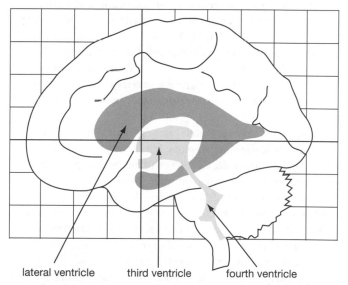

lateral ventricle   third ventricle   fourth ventricle

15. **Deep within the brain there are spaces filled with fluid (cerebrospinal fluid). These are called ventricles. There are two lateral ventricles, one within each of the two hemispheres. The third ventricle lies between the two cerebral hemispheres in the mid brain, and the fourth ventricle lies between the cerebellum and the brainstem. When the brain shrinks due to loss of tissue, as in Alzheimer's disease, the ventricles get larger. In patients with schizophrenia the ventricles tend to be slightly larger than normal (5%), but the reason for this increase in size is not known.**

There are, however, many unanswered questions. The possibility that the ventricular enlargement was due not to schizophrenia itself but to its treatment was raised early on because the chronically ill patients who were involved in the early investigations had often had extensive treatment, sometimes with insulin comas and multiple applications of electroconvulsive therapy as well as with antipsychotic drugs. Our study of matched patients, some of whom had and some of whom had not been exposed to various treatments, however, demonstrated that the enlargement of the ventricles was not due to these treatments. Nonetheless, we really do not know to what extent these brain changes are specific to schizophrenia. Such enlargements may well occur in other conditions, and we don't know when the enlargement occurs or what causes it. Many studies have tried to find a relationship between symptoms or course of the illness and the structural brain changes, but, on the whole, consistent findings have not been shown. The most robust results suggest that patients with enlarged ventricles are more likely to have general cognitive impairments and movement disorders.

CT scanning of the brain is still widely used for general clinical purposes, particularly in neurology, but for research purposes in relation to schizophrenia, CT has essentially been superseded by structural magnetic resonance imaging (MRI). The phenomenon of magnetic resonance imaging was originally described in the 1940s, but was not brought into clinical development until the late 1970s. In the 1980s the technique was first applied to schizophrenia and many studies have been conducted since. Lawrie and Abukmeil identified 40 relevant studies involving 1,314 patients with schizophrenia and 1,127 control volunteers. These studies confirmed the increase in size of the lateral ventricles and also revealed reductions in brain volume. Given the consistency of these results and the number of patients involved, there can be no real doubt that there is a small but replicable reduction in the overall brain size in patients with schizophrenia and that some areas of the brain show greater reductions than others. The most reduced areas seem to be the temporal lobes and the amygdala-hippocampal complexes (see Figure 16). We do not know how specific these changes are to schizophrenia; ventricular enlargement and reductions in brain size have sometimes been observed in patients with affective disorder.

When these abnormalities were first reported in the 1970s, the prevailing view was that they represented some form of degenerative change in the brain. This was supposed to follow some insult that took place around the time the patient first became ill. Various possibilities as to the nature of this acute insult were considered. For example, at one time it was suggested that some

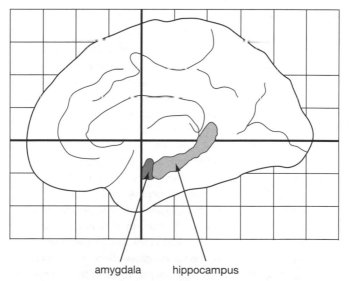

amygdala   hippocampus

16. The amygdala and the hippocampus are buried inside the temporal lobe in each hemisphere of the brain. The amygdala contains many components and is so called because it resembles an almond (Greek *amygdala*) in shape. The amygdala is concerned with emotion. The hippocampus is a complex structure that is so called because it is supposed to resemble a seahorse (Greek *hippocampus*). The hippocampus is concerned with long-term memory. In patients with schizophrenia, the amygdala and hippocampus tend to be slightly smaller than normal.

form of viral infection of the brain might underlie the condition. The suggestion from the CT scan studies that there might be degeneration in the brains of patients with schizophrenia reawakened interest in the neuropathology of brains of patients studied postmortem. If an insult, such as a viral infection, had occurred at the beginning of the illness, then signs of inflammation would be left in the brain in the form of gliosis, a kind of scar tissue that develops after damage to the brain. Gliosis can only be detected in brain tissue studied postmortem. A number of such studies have been performed, but no evidence of excessive gliosis in schizophrenics can be found.

Many researchers now consider that schizophrenia is a neurodevelopmental condition in which the basic abnormality arises very early in life, possibly in the foetus or around the time of birth. As a result of some sort of compensation, the abnormality does not lead to symptoms until early adult life. We do not know how this compensation might be achieved or why it finally breaks down. The idea that the nervous system has developed abnormally in people who will later develop schizophrenia can only be addressed if we can examine such people before they become ill. We know that abnormalities of brain structure are already present at the time of the first episode of schizophrenia, but it is difficult to scan people before the first episode because we have no way of knowing who is eventually going to get ill. One approach to this problem is to scan people who are currently well, but who are at high risk for developing schizophrenia because two or more close relatives have already received the diagnosis. Recent work in the Edinburgh High Risk Study suggests that many of these people do indeed show abnormalities of brain structure before the onset of the disorder. However, we do not know whether these abnormalities are specific to schizophrenia, or how they relate to the various signs and symptoms of the disorder.

Abnormalities of brain function

Imaging of the function of the brain has a shorter history than imaging of its structure. Development of SPECT (single photon emission computed tomography) and PET (positron emission tomography) has allowed blood flow to different regions of the brain to be assessed. The blood flow in a particular brain region is an index of the activity of the nerves in that region.

In 1974 Ingvar and Franzen observed that patients with schizophrenia had relatively reduced blood flow in the frontal regions of the brain when simply lying in the scanner 'at rest'. This 'hypofrontality' was particularly marked in the more deteriorated patients. Subsequently many studies of this kind have been conducted, and most, but not all, have observed similar results. Later work has tried to relate regional cerebral blood flow to cognitive processes, in particular to 'executive' processes such as planning (see Chapter 3), by having patients perform suitable tasks during scanning. In 1986 Weinberger and colleagues observed that medication-free patients with schizophrenia showed smaller increases of activity in the dorsolateral prefrontal cortex than controls while performing an executive task. There have been many subsequent studies of this type, and the result has not always been replicated. A few studies have even reported over-activity in the frontal cortex (hyperfrontality). In general, however, the results do suggest that there is reduced activity in the frontal lobes of patients with schizophrenia, both at rest and when performing tasks that normally elicit frontal activity. This abnormality is more likely to be found in patients with negative symptoms and does not seem to be a consequence of drug treatment.

Problems with the interpretation of studies of functional imaging

As we discussed in Chapter 3, patients with schizophrenia resemble patients with frontal lobe lesions in that they tend to perform badly on tests of executive function. It is therefore very tempting to conclude that the reduced frontal activity revealed by functional brain imaging studies reflects an abnormality of the frontal lobe. But this need not be the case. One problem with the functional imaging studies is that the schizophrenic patients often performed the tasks rather worse than the control subjects. Was the reduced frontal activity the cause of this poor performance, or the consequence of it? To resolve this problem we would need to look at the pattern of brain activity when the patient was performing better. This could be achieved by making the task easier or by waiting for the patient to recover from the current episode of illness. In either case, we would want to perform many more scans.

A more recent claim based on functional imaging studies is that there is reduced connectivity between the frontal lobes and more posterior regions of the brain in schizophrenia. However, connectivity between brain regions is difficult to assess unless we can record a great many scans. Furthermore, we would want to know whether connectivity is affected by drug treatment or symptom severity. Even more scans would need to be recorded to answer these questions.

Repeated scanning on this scale is simply not acceptable with techniques such as PET and SPECT that involve the use of ionizing radiation, particularly if young volunteers are involved. The possibility that there may be very long-term effects from even the small amounts of ionizing radiation involved may be remote, but it cannot be excluded. Given this problem the introduction of functional magnetic resonance imaging (fMRI) has been a major advance. fMRI uses magnetic resonance imaging to detect changes in blood oxygenation, which is a sign of a change in blood flow. As far as we know, this technique can be used as often as necessary in the same individual without any risk to their health. A number of fMRI studies have already been successfully carried out in patients with schizophrenia (see Chapter 7). In the next few years such studies should dramatically improve our understanding of brain function in schizophrenia.

Chapter 6
Environmental factors

As we have seen in the previous chapter, genetic factors have an important role in the cause of schizophrenia. But equally clearly genetic factors cannot be the whole story. Other factors must play a role. The search for these other factors has been wide-ranging and has gone on for a long time without a great deal of success. The factors may be divided into two broad classes: social/psychological and biological but not genetic.

The possibility of social/psychological causes of schizophrenia goes back to Freud and other psychoanalysts. Freud himself was primarily interested in neuroses rather than psychotic disorders, and the application of psychodynamic theories to psychotic people was largely carried out by his followers. Psychodynamic theories describe individuals as changing and developing rather than as static entities and assume that they are motivated by drives of which they may not be consciously aware. Psychodynamic accounts of psychosis can be divided into those that concentrate on the individual and those that concentrate on the family.

Can stress trigger an episode of schizophrenia?

A psychodynamic account of the development of psychosis in an individual depends upon trying to interpret the symptoms they describe against the background of what can be discovered about the formation of that individual's personality. The central assumption of this approach is that traumatic emotional events create psychological stress that causes the individual to regress to an earlier stage of emotional development. This regression can be associated with the appearance of psychotic symptoms. In some cases the individual adopts coping mechanisms for dealing with emotional stress, but as the emotional stresses accumulate, the coping mechanisms are finally overwhelmed and psychotic symptoms develop. The exact mechanisms underlying such sequences of events are not specified, but the clear assumption is that stressful events of some kind provide a trigger for the development of psychoses. This assumption leads to highly testable hypotheses, the most obvious being that individuals who develop schizophrenia have previously suffered more 'emotional stress' than individuals who do not become ill in this way. A large number of studies have been carried out to test this hypothesis.

In order to perform such studies it is necessary to decide in advance what sort of events are likely to cause emotional stress. One widely used scheme concentrates on 'life events'. These are events that occur in the lives of most people and are associated with major life changes. Such events can be positive as well as negative and include getting married, changing jobs, or the death of a family member. Studies of life events were pioneered by George Brown and Jim Birley in the late 1960s. They counted life events over a three-month period prior to the onset of an acute episode of illness in 50 patients with schizophrenia and in a control group of 325 matched healthy controls. In most cases the target episode of illness was not the first that the schizophrenics had experienced. In this study the patients encountered almost twice as many life events as the controls. Studies of this kind are difficult to interpret because it is possible that some life events (such as losing one's job) are the consequence rather than the cause of deteriorating health. The authors tried to exclude life events that obviously fell into this category, but it is difficult to eliminate the problem entirely.

Some, but not all, subsequent studies have replicated these findings. For example, Malzacher and colleagues did not find an unusually large number of life events in people prior to their first admission for schizophrenia. There probably is a role for stressful events in the onset of acute episodes of schizophrenia, but, as yet, the findings are suggestive rather than conclusive. In the Edinburgh High Risk Study we also found a relationship between major life stressors and psychotic symptoms. However, in this study also the result is difficult to interpret. Young people at enhanced risk of schizophrenia for genetic reasons were assessed before they become unwell and compared with a matched control group. In 2001, 39 of these high-risk subjects had developed psychotic symptoms, although they did not yet have a florid psychotic illness. Significantly fewer of the controls had such symptoms, but, in both the high-risk patients and the controls, those who had psychotic symptoms had also experienced more major life stressors. Because of our familiarity with the Edinburgh High Risk Study we are very much aware of the great difficulties of studies of this kind. We have observed that individuals who are at risk of developing schizophrenia show psychological impairments, fleeting hallucinations, and ill-sustained delusional beliefs on and off for years before they become sufficiently unwell to receive a formal diagnosis. Should we be counting life events prior to the time at which diagnosis is first received, or prior to the first appearance of these partial psychotic symptoms? How can we be sure that some life events are not a consequence of these transient psychotic symptoms?

Can a dysfunctional family cause schizophrenia?

Family theories of schizophrenia also arose from within the psychodynamic tradition. In the 1940s, a movement developed within this tradition that placed emphasis upon families as a whole than upon individual patients. In the case of schizophrenia it was suggested that symptoms developed as a reaction either to pathological relationships within the family or to abnormal patterns of communication within the family. The proponents of these theories used vivid terminology that has passed into general and literary usage. For example, in 1948, Frieda Fromm-Reichmann coined the phrase 'schizophrenogenic mother', and in 1956 Bateson put forward the 'double-bind' hypothesis.

Bateson suggested that, in some families, parents persistently communicate ambiguous and conflicting messages to their child. This pattern of communication would have a lasting effect upon the child, so that in later life such an individual might communicate in ways sufficiently aberrant to lead to a diagnosis of schizophrenia. Subsequent authors have elaborated this hypothesis. Lidz and colleagues suggested that abnormalities of parental relationships (marital skew and marital schism) could cause the child to be unable to interact with others outside the family in a normal way. Wynne and Singer raised the possibility that the child learned abnormalities of speech from his or her parents, so that as an adult he or she would have difficulty in interacting with others and might even think in ways that seemed illogical and inappropriate to others. These ideas underpinned the work of R. D. Laing, who wrote a number of books about schizophrenia, most notably *The Divided Self* and *Sanity, Madness and the Family*. He argued that schizophrenia is perhaps a reasonable response to an insane world. Laing writes vividly, and in *The Divided Self*, the plight of the patient whose communications cannot be understood by those concerned with her care is poignantly described:

Joan is a twenty-six-year-old woman. Her illness first appeared when she was seventeen. Joan was cold, withdrawn, seclusive, and suspicious. Visual and auditory hallucinations were active. She would enter into no hospital activities and frequently became so stuporous that it was difficult to elicit any response from her. If pressed about the need for treatment, she would become sullenly resistive or maintain angrily that she wanted to be left alone. Three suicidal attempts were made, by slashing herself with broken glass or by taking an overdose of sedation. Joan says '*We schizophrenics say and do a lot of stuff that is unimportant, and then we mix important things in with all this to see if the doctor cares enough to see them and feel them'.* Joan gives other examples: *"Patients laugh and posture when they see through the doctor who says he will help but really won't or can't. Posturing, for a girl, is seductive, but it's also an effort to distract the doctor away from all her pelvic functions. The patients try to divert and distract him. They try to please the doctor but also confuse him so he won't go into anything important. When you find people who will really help, you don't need to distract them. You can act in a normal way. I can sense if the doctor not only wants to help but also can and will help'.*

Joan gives examples of some ways in which the schizophrenic tries to conjure up assurances of being real from the awareness of being seen, and hence at least being *there*. The schizophrenic cannot sustain this conviction from inner sources.

Patients kick and scream and fight when they aren't sure the doctor can see them. It's a most terrifying feeling to realize that the doctor can't see the real you, that he can't understand what you feel and that he's just going ahead with his own ideas. I would start to feel that I was invisible or maybe not there at all. I had to make an uproar to see if the doctor would respond to me, not just to his own ideas.

Throughout her account, this patient repeatedly contrasts her real self with a compliant self which is false. The split between her 'real self' and her body is expressed vividly in the following passage:

If you had actually screwed me it would have wrecked everything. It would have convinced me that you were only interested in pleasure with my animal body and that you didn't really care about the part that was a person. It would have meant that you were using me like a woman when I really wasn't one and needed a lot of help to grow into one. It would have meant you could only see my body and couldn't see the real me which was still a little girl. The real me would have been up on the ceiling watching you do things with my body. You would have seemed content to let the real me die. When you feed a girl, you make her feel that both her body and her self are wanted. This helps her get joined together. When you screw her she can feel that her body is separate and dead. People can screw dead bodies, but they never feed them.

Her 'real self' had to be the starting point for the development of genuine integral status. This 'real self', however, was not readily accessible, both because of the dangers threatening it:

My interviews were the only place where I felt safe to be myself, to let out all my feelings and see what they were really like without fear that you would get upset and leave me. I needed you to be a great rock that I could push and push, and still you would never roll away and leave me. It was safe for me to be bitchy with you. With everyone else I was trying to change myself to please them.

17. The existential Glaswegian psychiatrist, R D Laing (1927–1989) developed a romantic account of schizophrenia as the response to intolerable stresses in the family and society, but which could lead, in the right circumstances to benefit and redemption.

but also because it was felt to be so charged with hatred and destructive potential that nothing could survive that entered into it.

Unfortunately, vivid and poignant descriptions are not enough. Hypotheses must be developed and examined scientifically. The 'double bind' hypothesis and its variants have not stood up to experimental scrutiny. Wynne and Singer's studies of the parents of people with schizophrenia are good examples of careful experiments. The authors argued that, if schizophrenia is caused by aberrant communication in the parents, then it should be possible to distinguish between the speech of these parents and the speech of parents of people with other disorders. They made transcripts of the speech of parents of people with schizophrenia and the speech of other parents. On the basis of these transcripts it was frequently possible to identify which were the parents of patients with schizophrenia. Wynne and Singer devised a measure of 'communication deviance'; these scores were substantially higher in the parents of schizophrenic patients. In 1975 Steven Hirsch and Julian Leff tried to replicate this work but were not able to do so. Although the communication deviance score was higher in the parents of the schizophrenic patients, there was a very substantial overlap between their scores and the scores of other groups. Furthermore, Hirsch and Leff found that the differences were almost all due to a small number of parents who had very high deviance scores. They examined the transcripts of these parents in more detail and found that these parents spoke much more than the other parents. When this greater amount of speech was taken into account, the parents of schizophrenic patients no longer showed higher deviance scores.

This observation fits in with clinical experience. Parents of young people with schizophrenia often do talk a lot to health service personnel, but then they have a great deal to talk about. Today, very little of this kind of work on families is carried out. To be the parent of a patient with schizophrenia causes enough suffering without the added distress of being told, on the basis of little evidence, that you may be the cause of the breakdown. The rise of relative support groups such as the National Schizophrenia Fellowship and their increasing ability to find a voice has made it very clear just how hurtful these ideas have been to many people.

The effects of an impoverished environment on the symptoms of schizophrenia

Psychodynamic theories about the causes of schizophrenia have not, on the whole, paid much attention to the range of different symptoms associated with the disorder. Unresolved conflicts, stresses, and in particular reactions to abnormal patterns of communication within the home are evoked to explain negative symptoms such as social withdrawal and difficulties in forming relationships with others as well as positive symptoms such as hallucinations and delusions.

Outside the domain of psychoanalysis, however, there is a large body of work proposing that social factors may have a specific role in the development of negative symptoms in schizophrenia. This work is largely concerned with the effects of institutional care. The idea is that the inevitable poverty of life in an institution will at least intensify and may even create the social withdrawal and lack of motivation seen in patients with schizophrenia.

Russell Barton wrote a monograph in 1959 entitled 'Institutional neurosis' in which he described the abnormalities that can be observed in people who have been in mental hospitals or other restricted environments for long periods of time. He mentioned features such as apathy, social withdrawal, deterioration of personal habits, and the adoption of peculiar postures, and suggested that these would arise in anyone who lived for a long time in a very restricted environment. However, the people he chose to observe were in fact patients with schizophrenia in Shenley Hospital in Hertfordshire, the same hospital in which we and our colleagues carried out much of our own early work on schizophrenia. The features Barton identified as typical results of living in an institution were rather similar to those we had observed as typical of chronic schizophrenia. The problem, as Barton appreciated, was how to separate out the effects of living in an institution from the effects of the illness.

The best-known work on institutionalization and the development of negative symptoms is that of John Wing and George Brown. Wing and Brown compared three mental hospitals that varied considerably in the degree of social stimulation that they offered. They found that patients in the hospital with the lowest level of social stimulation had the highest level of negative symptoms. Their observations suggest that a proportion, and it might be a substantial proportion, of the negative symptoms shown by long-stay patients in mental hospitals could be a product of their environment. Wing and Brown emphasized that they did not consider that institutionalism occurs solely in mental hospitals.

> Indifference about leaving lies at the very heart of institutionalism and we would expect to find it developing in the inmates of most total institutions, particularly in those from vulnerable groups such as the physically handicapped, mentally retarded or those with inadequate personalities. Schizophrenic patients are probably particularly at risk because of their vulnerability.

Wing and Brown also recognized the problem of separating the effects of institutionalization from the effects of schizophrenia.

> In long-stay patients these elements, clinical and social poverty, and 'institutionalism' often occur together and it may then seem difficult to disentangle the elements. However, secondary impairment develops in patients who have only mild to moderate clinical symptoms the longer they stay in hospital . . . thus institutionalism in mental hospitals should be regarded as no different in principle from the condition that develops in other institutions, although it may be seen in its more severe form in long-stay schizophrenic patients.

Although their study is entirely concerned with patients with schizophrenia living in the three hospitals that were compared, the authors believe, like Barton, that the effects they observed would be seen in anyone forced to live in an institution. This is clear from the quotation placed at the front of the book:

> Witness 1
> You could only react normally
>   during your first hours in the camp
> When you had been there any length of time
>   it was no longer possible
> You were absorbed into the routine
>   you were in prison
> And you had to make do
>
> Peter Weiss, *The Investigation*, Canto 2

In order to disentangle the effects of institutionalization from the effects of schizophrenia, it is not sufficient to look at patients with schizophrenia in an institution. We need to study patients with schizophrenia who are not in an institution and we also need to study people in an institution who are not suffering from schizophrenia. These important additional groups were examined in a series of studies by Eve Johnstone and David Owens. We carried out a survey of all of the patients in Shenley Hospital who had schizophrenia and who had been there for more than a year. There were 510 of them and the deficits that they had were substantial. We compared these patients with two additional groups: (1) patients with schizophrenia who had not received long-term in-patient care, and (2) patients who had received long-term in-patient care in Shenley Hospital but didn't have schizophrenia (they had manic-depressive psychosis). The results were clear. Both negative and positive features were equally severe in the two groups of patients with schizophrenia, while these features were less severe in the patients with manic-depressive psychosis. Indeed, the patients with manic-depressive psychosis showed a different pattern of behaviour from those with schizophrenia. The schizophrenic patients were more likely to behave as if they were hallucinated and engage in apparently pointless repetitive behaviour, while the manic depressives were more likely to be overactive, changeable, and at times to act in a hostile or destructive way. In other words, severe negative (and positive) features were associated with schizophrenia rather than institutionalization. One feature that did relate to institutionalization was cognitive impairment. Both groups of institutionalized patients were equally cognitively impaired, while the schizophrenic patients who were not in an institution were less impaired. These results suggest that positive and negative symptoms are likely to be continuing features of schizophrenia whether or not the patient is in an institution. Institutional care might be associated with worse cognitive deficits, but there was no evidence that it increased the other abnormalities. These conclusions were supported by work carried out by Curzon and colleagues, who found no relationship between the poverty of the social environment in an institution and negative features of schizophrenia such as blunted affect, social withdrawal, and poverty of speech.

No one would deny that an impoverished environment is detrimental for schizophrenic patients. Furthermore, most authors would agree that such environments could well exacerbate the deficits characteristic of schizophrenia. The tragedy is that for many patients today the social and material poverty associated with 'care in the community' may well be greater than they would have experienced in the better institutions of the past.

Biological factors in the early environment of patients with schizophrenia

Social and emotional stressors are not the only environmental factors that might be relevant to schizophrenia. Claims have also been made about a number of biological factors in the individual's early environment that might increase the risk of developing schizophrenia several years later. These claims are generally based on epidemiological studies.

Epidemiologists study patterns of disease in very large groups of people. If it is found that a disease occurs more frequently in one place than in another, this can give clues about what is causing the disease. The most famous example of this approach occurred during a cholera outbreak in London in the 1850s. John Snow noticed that people were more likely to get cholera if they lived near a particular water pump in Broad Street. From this observation, he correctly deduced that the water from that pump was contaminated and was causing the disease. More recently, epidemiological methods have provided clues about the causes of a number of disorders, such as multiple sclerosis and kuru, a disease that occurs in New Guinea and is similar to Creutzfeldt-Jakob disease.

Epidemiological methods work best when the frequency of disease varies from place to place and can be related to environmental factors that occur in some places and not others. There are a number of common diseases which, while they have a genetic element, nevertheless occur more frequently in some places. Examples of this would be diabetes and heart disease. These disorders have a genetic component, but are also affected by diet, cigarette smoking, and other non-genetic factors. It is well established that heart disease is much more frequent in Western Europe, and in places with Western diets and habits, than it is in other parts of the world. Schizophrenia is unusual in that there is very little variation in the incidence of this disorder from one place to another. Nevertheless, some robust results have emerged from epidemiological studies of schizophrenia. Although we are not able to interpret this evidence at the present time, these results may eventually lead to a better understanding of the causes of schizophrenia.

Some aspects of schizophrenia are affected by gender. Many studies have shown that the average age of onset in men is about five years earlier than that in women. The two sexes have also been shown to differ in the course of the illness in more general terms. Women seem to have functioned better before the onset of the illness and are less disabled afterwards. It is possible that women only appear to do better than men because society expects less from them, but it is hard to see how social expectations could affect age of onset. One suggestion is that the illness takes a more benign form in women through effects of oestrogens (female sex hormones) on dopamine D_2 receptors.

Another robust finding is the 'season of birth effect'. People who will go on to develop schizophrenia are more likely to be born in the winter. This finding was first reported by Tramer in 1929, but has since repeatedly been demonstrated both in the northern and southern hemispheres. We do not yet know what this effect means. One possibility is that there is some harmful agent that acts on the foetus in the womb or around the time of birth in such a way as to cause the later development of schizophrenia. This might be an agent that is more active in the winter and affects children once they are born, or it might be an agent that is active in the summer and autumn and affects mothers, and thus their infants, during pregnancy. Possible agents of this kind would include infectious diseases, extreme temperatures, or malnutrition.

If a mother is affected by influenza during the middle trimester of pregnancy, there is some evidence that her child is more likely to develop schizophrenia many years later. Most of this work relates to the 1957 influenza pandemic and has been investigated using data sets from Denmark, Scotland, England, and Wales. Unfortunately, much of the evidence linking influenza and schizophrenia in these studies is rather indirect. It was found that the children of mothers who were pregnant during 'flu epidemics were more likely to develop schizophrenia, but it is not known whether or not these particular mothers were actually affected by the virus. In a few studies it was possible to make a direct comparison of the children of mothers who were reported to have had 'flu and those of mothers who did not, and in these studies there was no effect of 'flu on the later development of schizophrenia. However, it is entirely possible that some of the mothers in the later group had mild infections of which they were not aware.

The effect of maternal starvation on the later development of schizophrenia has also been investigated. Maternal starvation is, unfortunately, far from uncommon, but it generally occurs in circumstances in which reliable records relating to registration of births etc. are unavailable. However, in Holland during the Second World War, there was considerable shortage of food during the winter of 1944/45, and during that time record keeping was maintained. Food deprivation was severe, but was circumscribed in time. An increased rate of schizophrenia was later found in the female offspring of women who were severely deprived of food during the first three months of their pregnancy. Both influenza and food deprivation would give rise to the later development of schizophrenia by affecting the brain during a critical stage of its development.

Many studies have asked whether difficulties around the time of birth can lead to the later development of schizophrenia. When data from these studies is pooled, it appears that babies who experience birth complications are twice as likely to develop schizophrenia as adults as those whose births are normal. However, there are a number of unsatisfactory features of these studies. In many cases the information about the birth complications came from the mothers' recollection of what happened. It is known that mothers are more likely to 'remember' and report birth complications for children who have not developed normally. Such a bias will increase the apparent association between birth problems and schizophrenia. In some large studies using hospital records of birth complications, no relationship has been found with schizophrenia. Certainly, it is not clear which obstetric complications are relevant to the development of schizophrenia, and the mechanism by which they might exert an effect is unknown.

Thus, at the end of a considerable number of studies, relatively few facts emerge. The idea that social/psychological factors have a major influence in causing and maintaining schizophrenia was very popular at one time, and, indeed, such ideas have been the central theme of powerful books and films. Hypothesis-driven studies in this area have produced little positive support for these ideas, although because of methodological difficulties the influence of life events cannot be discounted. The non-genetic biological environmental factors fare rather better. We may not be able to understand the meaning of the season of birth effect or why the average age of onset in males is years earlier than that in females, but the replicability of these findings is telling us something about the nature of schizophrenia. If we could understand what it is, we would probably have a much clearer idea of what causes schizophrenia to develop. How the relevant environmental factors interact with the clear genetic factors described in Chapter 5 may well be important, but at present opinions in this area are speculative rather than evidence-based.

Chapter 7

Understanding the symptoms of schizophrenia

An abyss of difference

The negative features of schizophrenia, the loss of will and the poverty of thought, are associated with a tragic decline in intellectual and social function. But these are perhaps not the most striking features of the illness for those of us looking from the outside in. It is the delusions and hallucinations – the false beliefs and the false perceptions – that are seen as the signs of true madness and have been the subject of morbid curiosity from earliest times. What are we to make of the patient who believes he is St Peter reborn, or the one who claims that he can control the economy by repeating certain words? When patients give more detailed descriptions of their experiences, these can be even harder to understand. How can we make any sense of the person who says, 'I am thinking about my mother, and suddenly my thoughts are sucked out of my mind by a phrenological vacuum extractor, and there is nothing in my mind', or 'It is not me who is unhappy, but they are projecting unhappiness into my brain. They project upon me laughter for no reason'?

These reports are hard to understand because they are completely outside our own experience. As Kurt Jaspers put it, there is an 'abyss of difference' between psychosis and normal consciousness.

The profoundest difference ... seems to exist between that type of psychic life which we can intuit and understand, and that type which, in its own way, is not understandable and which is truly distorted and schizophrenic ... we cannot empathize, we cannot make them immediately understandable, although we try to grasp them somehow from the outside.

Our aim in this chapter is to show that it is possible to achieve some understanding of these experiences. Studies of normal conscious processes and their correlates in the brain have made great advances since Jaspers issued his pessimistic pronouncements. We are beginning to understand how these processes can go awry and lead to certain symptoms associated with schizophrenia. This understanding also gives us some idea of what it must be like to have such symptoms.

Explaining symptoms

This approach to the study of schizophrenia is rather different from that adopted in the studies we have discussed in the previous chapters. Those studies were concerned to find causes that would be relevant to all patients with a diagnosis of schizophrenia. In this chapter we are concerned with studies where the starting point is to find a cause of a particular symptom or class of symptoms such as auditory hallucinations. This approach allows for the possibility that different symptoms have different causes. Furthermore, the same cause might apply to such a symptom even if it is associated with a disorder other than schizophrenia.

One of the problems with the study of schizophrenia lies with the extraordinary diversity of the disorder. One patient may hear voices talking to her and about her, while another falsely believes that he is a relative of the queen and is being persecuted by MI5. They have the same diagnosis, but share no symptoms in common. This diversity has led some people to propose that there is no such disorder as schizophrenia. They suggest that the term refers to a ragbag of different disorders with no common underlying cause. However, this variety of manifestations can also occur within the same patient at different times.

This may be seen in the case of Mrs M, a patient of Eve Johnstone (see p. 128).

About the only thing in common between these two episodes is the fear expressed by the patient. During the first episode she described feeling her body being controlled by alien forces, but was coherent and did not report auditory hallucinations. During the second episode she was incoherent and hallucinating.

In this case we would expect different cognitive processes and different patterns of brain activity to be associated with these different manifestations of the disorder. By studying specific symptoms, rather than 'schizophrenia' as a whole, we may remove a major source of variability from our data and perhaps have a better chance of identifying key abnormalities. However, although we may get a cleaner picture by studying symptoms in isolation, it must be remembered that most patients show many different symptoms at the same time.

Auditory hallucinations

Auditory hallucinations are a common feature of schizophrenia, and these false perceptions typically take the form of voices talking to or about the patient. Where do these voices come from? It has been known for a long time that, at least in some cases, the 'voices' are the patient's own speech. In 1949 Gould investigated a patient who heard voices almost continuously. Gould discovered that she was also whispering most of the time and was able to amplify this subvocal speech with a microphone. By recording the speech he was able to show that the subvocal speech corresponded to the 'voices'.

Whisper: She knows. She's the most wicked thing in the whole wide

Mrs M

At the time of her first admission she appeared afraid and she said that she believed her husband was paying for evil things to happen to her. She believed that he was trying to cause her to have bowel cancer or kidney trouble, and said that she was afraid to go to sleep because she believed that devil worshippers would take her over while she was sleeping and would control her body completely. She described feeling that the movements of her body were being controlled by others, possibly devil worshippers. She expressed these ideas coherently and denied that she was having any auditory hallucinations. She recovered from this episode and was discharged from hospital.

However, she was re-admitted seven years later after she stopped taking her medication. Once again she appeared fearful. She said that she was afraid of the activities of the IRA and felt that the IRA might be in the ward, that individuals in the ward and on the street were in disguise. She persistently believed that the psychiatrist in the ward was her aunt and could not accept evidence that this was not the case. It was difficult to follow what she was saying, as at times the connection between one idea and another was not at all clear, as in, for example, 'I don't trust you – beating the system – the IRA and Switzerland is neutral – are you religious'. She would describe auditory hallucinations but not, on this occasion, passivity experiences, which she said that she did not have. She shouted out loud to auditory hallucinations, saying things like 'don't talk about crucifixion'.

world. The only voice I hear is hers. She knows everything. She knows all about aviation.

Audible speech: I heard them say I have a knowledge of aviation.

A similar case was reported by Green and Preston in 1981; they also amplified the whispering with a microphone.

Patient (whisper): If you're in his mind, you come out of there but if you're not in his mind you won't come out of there. You want to stay there.

Examiner: Who said that?

Patient (normal voice): Er she said . . .

Patient (whisper): I said that.

The patient was challenged that he was talking to himself

Patient (normal voice): No, I don't. (aside) What is it?

Patient (whisper): Mind your own business darling, I don't want him to know what I was doing.

Patient (normal voice): See that, I spoke to ask her what she was doing and she said mind your own business.

These are extreme cases in which the patient's subvocal speech is sufficiently overt that it can be amplified and transcribed. However, we all use inner speech when trying to remember a telephone number or doing mental arithmetic, and this inner speech need not be accompanied by any overt whispering or mouth movements. It is possible that hallucinations could be accompanied by such covert inner speech even though there were no detectable signs that the patient was speaking or muttering during the hallucinations. The problem is how to study inner speech when it cannot be observed directly.

Inner speech has been intensively studied since Alan Baddeley and Graham Hitch first proposed the idea of an articulatory loop. The articulatory loop is a mechanism for maintaining words in memory for a short period. In order to keep a phone number in mind for the time it takes to get to the phone, we typically repeat the number to ourselves using the articulatory loop. Two components are involved: we articulate the number subvocally (the mind's voice), and we maintain the sound of this articulation for a short time (the mind's ear). However, we have to repeat the process if the material is to be kept in mind for more than a few seconds. This repetition creates the articulatory loop. This verbal working memory system is used in many tasks other than remembering phone numbers. For example, you will use it if you think about the sounds of the words you are reading at this moment.

It is easy to interfere with the functioning of the articulatory loop by asking people to articulate (for example, to say *la la la la*) while they are trying to remember words. If hallucinations are really inner speech, then such procedures should also interfere with hallucinations. There is some evidence that procedures like humming or subvocal counting can indeed reduce the severity of hallucinations, but not all patients find this helpful and the effects tend to be short-lived.

Another approach is to present tasks that can only be solved using the articulatory loop. For example, if you pronounced M-T aloud, what word would you hear? (*empty*). If hallucinations involve the articulatory loop, then they should specifically interfere with performance of tasks of this kind. Ceri Evans and his colleagues found that patients who were prone to hallucinations did not perform especially badly on a wide range of tasks that engage components of the articulatory loop. However, these results are difficult to interpret, since we do not know what effect the performance of these tasks had on the hallucinations. Perhaps the hallucinations stopped while the tasks were being performed. It is also possible that hallucinations are a form of inner speech that does not involve the articulatory loop.

A third approach is to find physiological markers for the presence of inner speech. Philip McGuire and his colleagues looked at brain activity in normal volunteers while they generated inner speech and also while they imagined the sound of someone else speaking. During inner speech a region of the left frontal cortex became active. This area is also active during overt speaking. While the subjects were imagining someone else speaking these areas became even more active, along with the regions of left temporal cortex that are engaged when we hear speech.

If hallucinations involve some form of inner speech then we would expect to see activity in these brain areas whenever hallucinations occur. It is quite difficult to identify the brain activity specifically associated with hallucinations. First, we need to find patients in whom the 'voices' come and go every minute or so rather than speaking continuously or rarely. Second, the patient must be willing

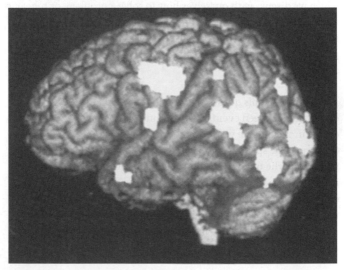

18. Location of brain activity associated with hallucinations. This patient experienced auditory and visual hallucinations (voices coming from heads that rolled around on the floor). Activity is seen in the visual and auditory association cortex. From Silbersweig et al. (1995).

to be scanned and be able to give a reliable indication of when the 'voices' are speaking. The small number of studies that have managed to find such patients have obtained largely similar results. During auditory hallucinations activity is seen in several brain regions, including areas involved in the reception and production of speech such as Broca's area. On the basis of an imaging study performed in 2000, Sukhi Shergill concluded that the pattern of activity occurring during hallucinations is remarkably similar to that observed when healthy volunteers deliberately imagine that another person is talking to them.

Self attribution

The idea that hallucinations are inner speech leads us to ask a rather different question about their cause. Inner speech in itself is not abnormal. Most normal thinking consists of inner speech in which we discuss with ourselves how to solve a problem, or rehearse to ourselves what we will say and what we expect others will say at some important meeting. So our new question is, why do patients perceive their inner speech as if it were coming from an outside source?

More generally this question is about how we make a distinction between events that we control (our inner speech) and events in the outside world that occur quite independently of us (someone else speaking). A problem with making this distinction might underlie not only auditory hallucinations, but also a number of other positive symptoms. The 'passivity' experiences emphasized by Kurt Schneider are so called because patients report that their actions, thoughts, and emotions are no longer caused by themselves, but imposed upon them by external agents.

> It is my hand and arm that move, and my fingers pick up the pen, but I don't control them. What they do is nothing to do with me. (Delusions of control)

The thoughts of Eamonn Andrews come into my mind. He treats my mind like a screen and flashes his thoughts on to it like you flash a picture. (Thought insertion)

In these examples the patients attribute the causes of their own actions and thoughts to an external agent. Something seems to have gone wrong with their ability to attribute their actions and thoughts to themselves.

Corollary discharge

The ability to distinguish between events caused by ourselves and independent events in the outside world is not something that is unique to humans. Any creature that is able to move its eyes has to solve the same problem. When we move our eyes the image of the world on the retina will move, but we do not experience the world jumping about. On the other hand, as Helmholtz pointed out in 1866, if we move our eye by poking it gently with our finger, then the world does appear to jump about. Normally when we move our eyes, the brain somehow suppresses the movement of the visual world that this generates. The principle of this mechanism was described by Helmholtz and many of the details have been elucidated since his time. The idea is that the effect of an eye movement on the visual world can be predicted on the basis of the command that was sent to the eye muscles to generate the movement. So, in addition to sending a message to the muscles, a corollary message (corollary discharge) is sent to the brain area that will be affected by the movement of the visual world created by the eye movement. The corollary discharge can cancel out the movement and thus the world will appear to stay still. This corollary discharge effectively labels the movement as self-generated and distinguishes it from movements happening independently in the outside world. This self-monitoring mechanism does not apply only to eye movements. There is suppression of the sound of our own voice when we speak and suppression of the sense of touch when we move our limbs.

19. Portrait of Hermann von Helmholtz (1821–94), physiologist and physicist. He was the first person to measure the speed with which electrical activity travels through nerves and was the inventor of the ophthalmoscope, an instrument used to examine the inside of the eye. He recognized that perception is a creative process dependent upon 'unconscious inferences' made in the brain.

If something went wrong with this self-monitoring system there would be two main consequences. At the psychological level, we would have difficulty distinguishing between events caused by our own actions and those occurring independently of us. At the physiological level, there would be overactivity in brain regions responding to the sensory consequences of our own actions.

A number of people have suggested that many of the positive symptoms of schizophrenia reflect a failure of some form of self-monitoring. As we shall see, the corollary discharge mechanism can readily be applied to symptoms like delusions of control. In this case, the patient is making overt movements and experiencing the sensations caused by those movements. It is not so easy to apply the model to symptoms like auditory hallucinations or thought insertion, as in these cases no overt behaviour is occurring and so there is no sensation to be suppressed. Irwin Feinberg has pointed out that inner speech and thought are internalized forms of action to which the corollary discharge model should apply. This idea potentially provides a unitary account for a whole range of positive symptoms – the problem is that these internalized processes are very difficult to study experimentally.

Delusions of control as a failure of self-monitoring

There is robust evidence that we are aware of the action we are about to perform before we actually perform it. The same mechanism allows us to imagine making a movement without any movement actually being performed. Imagining making movements can help us to improve our skills, while being aware of the movement we are about to make enables us to check that we are making the right movements very rapidly. The ability to imagine the movements we are about to make is a form of self-monitoring that may be related to corollary discharge. Patients with delusions of control and related symptoms have problems that suggest that they cannot monitor their own movements in the normal way.

A number of studies have shown that such patients are unable to make the rapid error corrections that depend upon self-monitoring. A recent study specifically examined the ability to imagine making movements. We all move more slowly when aiming for a smaller rather than a larger target. The same effect is seen even when we simply imagine aiming at a small target. Maruff and his colleagues found that patients with passivity symptoms did not show this change in timing when they imagined aiming at small targets, even though their real aiming speed showed the normal pattern.

By imagining the movement we are going to make, with all its sensory consequences, we are not at all surprised when these predicted consequences occur. This idea has been used to explain the well-known observation that we cannot tickle ourselves. Since we are making the tickling movements, we can predict exactly the sensations we will experience. Sarah-Jayne Blakemore has conducted a series of experiments on tickling to confirm this idea. In one experiment people tickled themselves via a robot arm that sometimes introduced delays between the movements the people made and the movements they felt. With delays of only 200 milliseconds the tickling sensation was as strong as if the person was being tickled by someone else. In this case, the delay has falsified the prediction and the damping down of the tickling sensation can no longer occur. Patients with passivity symptoms do not show the normal tickling pattern. For them, tickling themselves is as intense as being tickled by someone else. This observation is consistent with the idea that these patients are failing to predict the consequences of their actions; the sensory consequences of their actions are not damped down when processed by the brain.

Although a tickling experiment has yet to be performed, there is evidence for overactivity in the relevant brain areas when patients are simply moving a limb. Sean Spence scanned patients with delusions of control while they continuously moved a lever in various directions. These patients experienced their delusions while they were performing the task. They showed overactivity in the parietal cortex, a region known to be concerned with representing the position of the limbs in space. This overactivity was no longer observed when the patients had recovered from their delusions.

If self-monitoring is a more general failure underlying many positive symptoms then these other symptoms might also be associated with failure to damp down activity in brain regions associated with sensation. For example, if limb movements during delusions of control are associated with overactivity in the parietal cortex, then speaking during auditory hallucinations might be associated with overactivity in the temporal cortex, where sounds are analysed. Judy Ford and her colleagues used the electroencephalogram (EEG) to measure the brain activity elicited by irrelevant sounds while people were talking. In healthy controls responses to irrelevant sounds were reduced when they were talking, suggesting that the auditory cortex was damped down, but this effect was not seen in patients with schizophrenia. This is consistent with the idea that these patients were not able to damp down activity in their auditory cortex while they were speaking.

The disconnection hypothesis

The self-monitoring model assumes that the damping down of responses to sensations that we cause by our own actions results from signals coming from brain regions involved in generating the actions. It is well established that the frontal lobes are involved in generating action, so that it is plausible that the damping down seen in healthy volunteers depends upon interaction between the frontal cortex and posterior brain regions concerned with analysis of sensations. We have hypothesized that the overactivity seen in patients with delusions of control could be due to a failure of this interaction between the frontal cortex and the relevant posterior regions. In this particular case, the disconnection from the frontal cortex leads to overactivity of the parietal cortex, so that the patient is abnormally aware of limb movements. Other symptoms might be associated with overactivity in other regions. For example, we know that auditory hallucinations can be associated with activity in regions of the temporal cortex concerned with analysing speech. This overactivity might also result from functional disconnections between the frontal and temporal cortex.

A number of studies have attempted to measure the degree of connection between the frontal and temporal cortex using various brain imaging techniques. In a recent small-scale study using fMRI we observed reduced connectivity in patients who were generating words subvocally. This was related specifically to the severity of hallucinations they were currently experiencing: the greater the severity of the hallucinations, the more the connectivity was reduced.

Judy Ford and her colleagues used EEG to measure the degree to which frontal and temporal cortex were interacting during talking and listening. We would expect there to be more interaction during talking since, when talking, we can use the commands that generate the speech to predict and thereby damp down the sound of our own voice. In healthy controls there was increased interaction during talking as compared to listening. This effect was much reduced in patients with schizophrenia, particularly in the left hemisphere speech areas, and particularly in those patients prone to hallucinate.

We need much more evidence before we can be confident that a disconnection between brain regions underlies many of the positive symptoms of schizophrenia. However, this idea does have the considerable advantage that it can bridge the gap between psychological accounts of these symptoms and fundamental physiological processes in the brain.

What is it like to have delusions of control?

From most research papers concerned with the symptoms of schizophrenia the reader learns little more than that certain symptoms occurred in a proportion of patients with a particular severity ('10% of patients had definite delusions of control'). Few papers tell us what it is like to have delusions of control. In order to understand what these strange symptoms are like, it is helpful to be able to compare them with strange experiences reported by other patients who do not have a diagnosis of schizophrenia.

The anarchic hand sign is a rare disorder associated with discrete brain lesions. Patients with this disorder find that one of their hands (the one on the opposite side to the brain lesion) is no longer under their control. This anarchic hand grasps doorknobs or picks up a pencil and starts to scribble with it. Patients are upset by the actions of the hand: 'It will not do what I want it to do'. They will often try to prevent it from moving by grasping it firmly with the other hand. In one case, the patient's 'left hand would tenaciously grasp any nearby object, pull at her clothes, and even grasp her throat during sleep'. She slept with the arm tied to the bed to prevent such nocturnal misbehaviour.

The anarchic hand of these patients seems to be behaving like the hands of schizophrenic patients who have delusions of control. What the hand does is really 'nothing to do' with the patient. Nevertheless, anarchic hand patients do not typically say, 'Alien forces are controlling my hand'; instead, they say, 'There is something wrong with my hand. It will not do what I want it to do'. When we look at delusions of control more closely there are other striking differences. We already mentioned the study by Sean Spence in which patients with delusions of control were asked to perform a simple task in which they had to hold a lever and produce a random sequence of movements. They performed this task perfectly normally and yet they reported that alien forces were controlling their actions.

The contrast is striking. For patients with an anarchic hand, the hand is not doing what they want it to do and they try to stop it. For patients with delusions of control, the hand is doing what they want it to do and they do not try to stop it. So why do they feel that they are not in control of their actions? We have suggested that this question can be answered in terms of the self-monitoring model. Normally when we make a movement we predict the sensory consequences of that movement approximately 100 milliseconds before these sensations actually reach our brain. If the sensations do not match our prediction, then this is a signal that something unexpected has happened. Unexpected sensations indicate that we are not fully in control of our movements. Furthermore, unexpected sensations cause more brain activity than expected ones. If someone moves our arm (a passive movement) more activity is seen in the parietal cortex than if we make the same movement ourselves (an active movement).

So if something went wrong with this self-monitoring mechanism that predicts the consequences of our actions, then deliberate active movements might feel like unpredictable passive movements. The experience would be something like, 'My arm did what I intended, but it felt as if it was being moved by some external force.' Our suggestion, therefore, is that, for patients with delusions of control, active movements feel like passive movements. There is, however, a further consequence of the self-monitoring disorder that might explain another aspect of the experience of delusions of control. The patient is intending to make the movements, but when the movements are made they feel as if they are passive and being imposed by some external force. For this to happen this force must 'know' what these intended movements were to be. This is not some abstract physical force, but an agent that can read minds.

Imagine that you are playing a piano, but that the keys depress themselves just before your fingers move down. Perhaps it is a mechanical piano that happens to be playing the same tune. But then you find that it makes the errors that you make and, if you suddenly switch to a different tune, it anticipates those notes as well. Whatever agent it is that is controlling the piano, that agent is able to read your intentions. Perhaps this is what it is like to experience delusions of control.

Hallucinating other minds

The idea of self-monitoring defects was developed to explain those positive symptoms in which patients experience their own actions as being created by outside forces. Such symptoms include delusions of control, thought insertion, 'made' emotions, and so on. Our final account of the theory seems also to be relevant to another class of symptoms in which patients falsely believe that they are being influenced in various ways by other minds. Such symptoms would include the false belief that others are reading your mind (thought broadcasting), the false belief that others are communicating with you (delusions of reference), and the false belief that others are persecuting you (paranoid delusions). In all these cases, patients have 'hallucinated' a non-existent mind that interacts with them. So where do these other minds come from?

A number of studies have shown that many patients with schizophrenia have difficulty performing so-called 'theory of mind' tasks, in which they have to work out the intentions, wishes, or beliefs of other people. Our example comes from Rhiannon Corcoran's hinting task in which, if the husband says to his wife, 'This shirt is rather crumpled', he means 'will you please iron my shirt'. Many patients with schizophrenia are not able to work out that this is the intention behind the utterance.

However, having difficulty reading the intentions of others is not the same as seeing intentions when none are there. The next step in trying to understand the symptoms of schizophrenia will be to study how we normally distinguish between intentions and random events in the world around us. Our current speculation, hinted at above, is that this ability is intimately related to our experience of controlling our own actions. It is this experience that enables us to understand the intentions behind the actions of others.

Weird experiences are not enough

So far, our account of symptoms like delusions of control makes the fundamental assumption that these false beliefs are created by abnormal experiences. For the patient an active movement feels like a passive movement, and this is an abnormal experience. The patient has to explain this experience, and concludes that the movement must be being controlled by some external force. After all, passive movements are normally controlled by external forces. We assume that this is the explanation that we would all arrive at if we were having this strange experience.

The same approach underlies an extremely ingenious explanation of a rare and very striking symptom known as 'Capgras syndrome'.

This is the belief that a person has been replaced by an identical or almost identical other. The person who has been replaced is usually someone close to the patient, like a husband or wife. One interesting aspect of this symptom is that it can be observed in patients with known physical disorders such as Alzheimer's disease as well as in schizophrenia. Patients often act on this delusion by demanding that the 'impostor' should leave the house. In one extreme case, a patient who believed that his step-father had been replaced by a robot subsequently decapitated him to look for batteries and controls in his head.

This delusion is thought to result from an abnormal experience of faces. We know that the perception of faces depends upon at least two independent systems in the brain. One system allows us to recognize who the person is, while the other creates in us an emotional response to the person. Neurological patients with damage to visual areas of the brain sometimes lose the ability to recognize faces, even of people whom they know very well (this condition is called prosopagnosia). Yet they still show emotional responses, measured in terms of increased autonomic responses (sweating and heart rate), to these faces that they cannot recognize. Haydn Ellis and Andy Young have suggested that Capgras syndrome is the mirror image of prosopagnosia – the patient recognizes the face, but no longer experiences any emotional response to the person. They have confirmed that these patients do not show autonomic response to familiar faces. The patient is aware of the identity of the person in front of him, but, through the lack of an emotional response, feels that there is something fundamentally wrong. 'This person looks like my wife, but cannot really be her.' But is this abnormal experience really sufficient to justify the extremely unlikely conclusion that the wife has been replaced by a double? There is some evidence from patients with brain lesions that such delusions only occur after a combination of impairments. First, there must be damage to visual systems concerned with face recognition, so that the patient is not quite so good at recognizing faces as before. Second, there must be damage to the right frontal cortex, an area that seems to be involved in preventing us from adopting extremely unlikely hypotheses.

This idea that abnormal experiences are sufficient to cause delusions can be tested by presenting normal people with abnormal experiences. We attempted to do this by distorting the sound of people's voices. The volunteers were rigged up with a throat microphone and earphones. The speech recorded by the microphone was played into special-effects equipment where it could be distorted before being played back into the earphones. All this happened without any detectable delay, so that the volunteer heard their own voice at a different pitch. So, for example, a male speaker might hear his voice at a higher pitch, like the voice of a woman. We did this with patients during an acute episode of schizophrenia, asking them to speak while we altered the pitch of the voice in various ways. The comments they made were rather surprising.

> A female voice doesn't sound like me. It only speaks when I speak. Sounds like the sounds a deaf person might make.

> The voice has changed to a masculine voice. Same as a deaf masculine voice. I think it's an evil spirit speaking when I speak.

Patients who were suffering from delusions at the time of the experiment were very likely to attribute the voice they heard to another person, but only when the voice was distorted. On the other hand, our healthy volunteers and patients not reporting delusions would correctly attribute the voice to themselves. 'It's my voice I can hear, but you've done something to it with that box.'

This study shows that weird experiences are not enough. Only the patients who were concurrently experiencing delusions thought the voice they heard belonged to someone else.

Many of the delusions reported by patients with schizophrenia seem to result from a combination of an abnormal experience with a willingness to develop extremely unlikely explanations for that experience.

Does understanding lead to treatment?

Much progress has been made in our understanding of the psychological and physiological processes underlying the abnormal experiences associated with schizophrenia. Is there any way that this understanding of symptoms can lead to improvements in treatment? We have already discussed the enormous impact of drug treatment on schizophrenia in Chapter 4. The vast majority of patients are treated with drugs, and large sums of money are spent by the pharmaceutical industry in developing new drug treatments. As noted already, although these drugs are not wholly satisfactory, the evidence from controlled clinical trials of their value both in the treatment of acute schizophrenic episodes, and on a maintenance basis to prevent the symptoms returning, is overwhelming. In the last few years, however, there has been increasing interest in developing psychological treatments for schizophrenia that target particular signs or symptoms. Many of these treatment packages are targeted at the negative features of schizophrenia (where the evidence for the value of drug treatments is much weaker) and aim to improve particular functions such as social interactions, planning, memory, and attention. On the face of it, this approach would seem straightforward and helpful. Somewhat surprisingly, therefore, a recent review of many studies by Stephen Pilling and his colleagues found no evidence that such approaches were of any value whatever. In contrast, psychological treatments targeting specific positive symptoms involving misperceptions and false beliefs do seem to be of some value.

If we gain some understanding of the symptoms of schizophrenia, then we can use this understanding to devise psychological treatments. If hallucinations derive from subvocal articulation of which the patient is unaware, then deliberately articulating should suppress the hallucinations. Various simple techniques have been tried, including humming, subvocal counting, reading aloud, or naming the objects in a room. All these techniques seem to help some patients, but they have to be used continuously, which is not always practical. If hallucinations involve the auditory system in a more general way, then they should be suppressed if the patient has to use the auditory system for some competing task. Here, too, a number of simple techniques have been tried such as listening to music or to news or discussion programmes. These techniques also seem to work for some patients, but the material they are listening to has to be interesting. Listening to a boring voice is not helpful, while listening to random noises can actually make the hallucinations worse.

Psychological explanations of hallucinations, and many other symptoms, propose that these depend upon false beliefs held by the patients – that the voices they hear come from external agents, that alien forces are controlling their movements, or that people are trying to communicate with them. Cognitive behaviour therapy (CBT) is specifically aimed at altering beliefs and attitudes. This approach has had some success in treating depression by, for example, decreasing the frequency of negative thoughts and increasing the frequency of positive ones.

CBT has been used to challenge the beliefs underlying auditory hallucinations and other symptoms and has achieved success in many cases. An interesting example is the study by Peter Chadwick and Max Birchwood from 1994. The distressing thing about auditory hallucinations is not so much hearing voices per se, but what the voices say. Frequently, the voices tell patients to do and believe unpleasant things, and they may threaten that terrible things will happen if their commands are not obeyed. In their therapy, Chadwick and Birchwood did not challenge the existence of the voices. If you are clearly hearing a voice, how can I, who have no access to your mind, prove that it is not real? Instead, they challenged the threats made by the voices. Patients were encouraged to test these threats and prove to themselves that nothing terrible happened when they refused to obey the voices. Some patients are clearly helped by this approach, and the effects seem to last after treatment is finished. As our understanding of the symptoms of schizophrenia increases, it should be possible to devise better psychological treatments that specifically take account of the psychological processes underlying symptoms.

The development of new drug treatments should also be aided by discoveries about the processes underlying specific symptoms. For example, if it can be confirmed that some symptoms are associated with reduced interactions between brain areas, it may be possible to identify physiological mechanisms that control the extent of interactions and to develop drugs that specifically target these mechanisms. Such approaches are currently being explored, although effective treatments derived in this manner may be some way off.

Chapter 8
The importance of schizophrenia

What are we afraid of?

Over the last hundred years there has been a dramatic increase in the scientific understanding of severe mental illnesses like schizophrenia. Our purpose in this book has been to outline these developments in our understanding. We now know that schizophrenia is fundamentally a biological problem that is no different in principle from other such problems, like cancer or heart disease or diabetes. We know that schizophrenia is not caused by possession by evil spirits, or by a weak personality, or a bad mother. Yet in spite of all this knowledge, we remain deeply fearful of all mental illnesses and of schizophrenia in particular. In many ways we are right to be afraid. Schizophrenia can be a deeply unpleasant and distressing disorder that causes great suffering not only to the patient, but also to his or her family and friends. But our fear of schizophrenia is different from our fear of long-term debilitating problems like rheumatoid arthritis or multiple sclerosis. In this chapter we shall explore the reasons for this fear and suggest that understanding schizophrenia has wide implications for understanding the human condition in general.

Losing one's mind

We are especially frightened by the thought of having a mental illness ourselves. This fear is manifest in the various euphemisms that we use. We still talk of 'having a nervous break down' or 'suffering from over work'. We avoid saying that someone is suffering from schizophrenia or has a mental illness perhaps because such labelling might upset them too much and stigmatize them in the view of other people, or perhaps because we just don't like to be too specific about such things. The uncle who spent many years in mental hospitals is expunged from family history. In contrast, people with physical illnesses are often the focus of their families' concern and are admired for the dignity of their suffering. What is the difference?

If part of our body is damaged or removed this does not affect our personality or our ability to behave as a rational human being. The idea of losing our mind, however, carries with it the idea that we will also lose precisely those faculties that distinguish us as humans from other animals – the ability to think rationally, the ability to distinguish the true from the false, the ability to distinguish right from wrong, the ability to share experiences – everything really that makes us ourselves. This attitude to madness is expressed in the many different phrases that are used colloquially. Phrases like 'off his trolley', 'daft as a brush', 'not all there', and 'barking mad' all express the idea that the mad person is no longer rational, and in the case of 'barking mad' has been reduced to the state of an animal. This is the kind of attitude that provides justification for excluding the mad from human society and treating them, however kindly, like children or animals. Until very recently people detained in long-stay mental hospitals could, like convicted criminals, be denied the right to vote. The reasons for this were clearly revealed in a parliamentary debate on the subject in January 2000.

> I was always under the impression that the reason why people in mental hospitals were excluded from the right to vote was that it was held that they were not capable of making a rational decision.
>
> Mr William Ross (East Londonderry)

20. The terror of madness: poster of Olivia de Havilland in *The Snake Pit*.

Those of us outside, of course, do not have to pass any test of rationality, or indeed of any other kind, to exercise that right. The fear of becoming mad is partly the fear of being excluded from society. But there is also a more fundamental fear generated by the mere existence of madness.

How do I know what's real?

Ninety-nine per cent of the time we go through our lives untroubled by problems of reality. It never occurs to us to doubt that the world we perceive through our senses is the real world, the same world that is perceived by everyone else. Such certainty is denied the patient with schizophrenia. The person who is hallucinating is having perceptual experiences that are not part of the real world as experienced by everyone else. The voices he hears are not 'out there', but in his mind. And yet he is convinced that they are real. 'L. Percy King' is the pseudonym of a patient who sent a 20,000-word letter to the psychology clinic at Harvard University in the early 1940s. Mr King heard the voices of people who pursued him at a distance.

> I could see them nowhere, [but] I heard one of them, a woman, say, 'You can't get away from us: we'll lay for you, and get you after a while!' To add to the mystery, one of these 'pursuers' repeated my thoughts aloud, verbatim.

He developed a most ingenious account of how these voices were being transmitted.

> These pursuers are also able to project their magnetic voices along a water pipe, which acts as an electrical conductor by talking against it so that their voices seem to issue from the water running from the faucet connected to the pipe. One of them is able to make his voice roar along the large water mains for miles, truly a startling phenomenon. Most persons do not dare mention such things to their associates for fear of being judged insane.

Mr King knew all about insanity and the importance of hallucinations.

> Let me give you the original legal definition of insanity, which is: 'An insane person is one who cannot tell the difference between right and wrong.' . . . The 'Knowledge of right and wrong' referred to in this legal definition appertains solely to delusions, orientation, hallucinations. . . . Persons who have hallucinations of hearing *imagine* they hear things.

Mr King's logic is impeccable. He is not imagining. He is hearing real voices and therefore he is not insane.

What this example, and the many others like it, makes clear to us is that there is nothing intrinsic to the hearing of a voice (or any other experience) that enables us to know whether it is real or imaginary. The occurrence of hallucinations reveals to us that our hold on reality is very tenuous. What makes us so sure that the world we are experiencing is not simply the creation of our own disordered minds?

I think, therefore I am

Philosophers have worried about this problem at least since Plato. In Plato's dialogue *Theaetatus*, Socrates says,

> There still remains to be considered an objection which may be raised about dreams and diseases, in particular about madness, and the various illusions of hearing and sight, or of other senses. For you know that in all these cases the 'esse is percipi' (to be is to be perceived) theory appears to be unmistakably refuted, since in dreams and illusions we certainly have false perceptions; and far from saying that everything that we see exists, we would rather say that nothing that we see exists.

'Esse is percipi' is a phrase coined by Bishop Berkeley, the

philosopher who worried whether the tree would still be there when no one was looking at it. He promoted the idealist position that the reality of things is created by minds. 'Things only exist in consequence of being perceived.' In other words, the tree only exists because we see it. Through Socrates, Plato is making the point that we cannot rely on our senses in this way to define reality. If we make this assumption then the things that madmen see are just as real as the things that we see. But we know that the perceptions that occur in madness, and in dreams, are false.

Consideration of this problem was the starting point that led to Descartes' famous aphorism, 'I think, therefore I am'. Descartes was trying to deduce what, if anything, there was in our experience that we could be sure about. We can't be sure of our senses because, as the existence of hallucinations shows, these sights and sounds might be created in our brains (Descartes imagined that they were created by a malicious demon). Likewise, our memories of the past might have been created a few seconds ago. All that is left for us to be sure about, Descartes concludes, is the existence of our thinking selves.

Contemporary philosophers refer to a version of this idea as 'immunity to error through misidentification', or the 'immunity principle'. If a person says that she has a toothache, then, philosophers claim, it makes no sense to ask her, 'Are you sure it is *you* that is having the toothache?' If she says, 'I am trying to lift my arm', it makes no sense to ask her, 'Are you sure that it is *you* that is trying to lift your arm?'

But even this small island of security in the sea of uncertainty is undermined by some of the experiences reported by patients with schizophrenia. As John Campbell puts it,

> What is so striking about the phenomenon of thought insertion as described by schizophrenic patients is that it seems to involve an error of identification. . . . A patient who supposes that someone

else has inserted thoughts into his mind is right about which thoughts they are, but wrong about whose thoughts they are.

Likewise, the patient who states that when he moves his arm, it is not him that is moving it (delusion of control) is right about the movement of the arm, but wrong about who is doing the moving.

Confronted with this problem, philosophers have suggested that immunity to error can still be preserved if we make the distinction between agency and ownership of thoughts and actions. The patient with delusions of control is wrong about the agency of the arm movement since it is not someone else who is moving his arm. However, he is right about the ownership, since he knows that it is his arm that is moving.

Of course, the great majority of us do not experience hallucinations or delusions of control. Most of the time we have no doubt that what we experience is real and that we are in control of our actions. The existence of madness reminds us how fragile this certainty is. The idea of madness is frightening because it reminds us that our minds are essentially alone in an uncertain world.

Shared delusions

What the existence of hallucinations tells us is that there is no direct way of knowing whether our perception is caused by some event in the real world that impinges on our senses or by activity occurring spontaneously in the brain. Indeed, direct electrical stimulation can create perceptual experiences in people who are not psychotic (see Lee et al., 2000 in the References). So how do we know so confidently which experiences relate to the real world and which do not?

The most important feature of reality is that it is the same for all of us. If there is a real world out there, it remains roughly the same whoever is looking at it. The best way of checking the reality of our perceptions is to confirm that they correspond to the experiences of everyone else. This mutual checking applies not only to what we experience with our senses, but also to those things we believe about the world that are not based directly on our senses. Our view of reality can be conceived of as a mass delusion; 500 years ago we 'knew' that the Earth was flat, now we know it is round.

One of the problems for people with schizophrenia is that their perceptions and beliefs are no longer appropriately constrained by the perceptions and beliefs of other people. Patients with bizarre beliefs are not irrational – they can justify their beliefs. There was a 56-year-old patient in Shenley who claimed to be six weeks old. Questioned by Eve Johnstone that this surely could not be right as she could walk and talk and do things for herself, she replied 'I am very advanced'. The kinds of justification given are often quite skilful. For example, Alan Baddeley and his colleagues describe a patient who believes he is a Russian chess Grand Master.

> But if you don't speak Russian, isn't that rather odd for a Russian chess player?

> Yes, well, I don't speak Russian, but I think it's possible that I've been hypnotised to forget things like the fact that I can speak Russian.

This justification is very unlikely, but not logically impossible. What makes the TV series *The X-Files* such a successful example of the horror genre is that Mulder's paranoid beliefs and the convoluted explanations he develops for them always turn out to be true. This madman sees the world as it is and we, the sane, are deluded.

Because so many of our beliefs depend upon the culture we share with others, diagnosing patients from other cultures raises many problems. If hearing voices talking to you is a widely shared experience within a culture, then this experience cannot be treated as a sign of schizophrenia. On the other hand, people from within the same culture can easily recognize the kind of experiences that would be considered signs of madness.

In Northwick Park Hospital there were many patients who were adherents of religions with which the staff were not familiar – fundamental Christian sects as well as branches of oriental faiths. We could not be sure if it was reasonable for a man belonging to a Christian sect founded in California in 1962 to believe that by wearing a half-pound cross on a wire round his neck he pleased God, who would then pass him messages by directing his eyes to particular biblical texts. We could not be sure if it was reasonable for a devout Hindu to interpret individuals and animals in the local setting as manifestations of Krishna reborn. Reading accounts of the beliefs of adherents to these sects did not help us, but the relevant spiritual leaders, on the basis of a few moments' conversation, could state with confidence that these ideas were due to illness. We therefore made a practice of always consulting them. Typically they considered that the patient believed literally in what was intended as a metaphor. The patients' ideas were much too concrete.

But this cultural definition of delusions brings with it many dangers. When everyone believes the world is flat, is Columbus mad because he believes the world is round? When everyone believes in the inevitable triumph of communism, is it madness rather than political dissidence to believe otherwise? This view seems to have been held by many Soviet psychiatrists.

> The patient's mental illness has recurred; his counterrevolutionary statements are none other than a pathological mental symptom of his longstanding reactionary views. Diagnosis: schizophrenia.

Occasionally, the sharing of the experiences and beliefs that make our reality can create delusions in people who are probably normal. In cases of folie à deux two people share the same psychotic delusions. The two people are usually closely related and somewhat isolated from the rest of society. It is often the case that there is a dominant member of the pair who has schizophrenia, while the other seems to be normal. The normal member has come to share the psychotic delusions. When the pair is separated, the non-dominant member ceases to hold the delusions.

Even more rarely a strong personality with psychotic delusions is able to impose them on a whole community. This seems to have been the case in the tragic 'Jonestown massacre'.

> On November 18, 1978, in a cleared-out patch of Guyanese jungle, the Reverend Jim Jones ordered the 911 members of his flock to kill themselves by drinking a cyanide potion, and they did.

Jim Jones was the charismatic leader of a religious cult. He was almost certainly psychotic. He suffered from mysterious fainting spells, heeded advice from extraterrestrials, practised faith healing, and experienced visions of a nuclear holocaust. He led his followers to a remote part of the Guyanese jungle, where they set up a community isolated from the rest of society. The community lived in fear of an unnamed enemy and destroyer who would descend upon them and kill them mercilessly. The mass suicide occurred after the visit of a US Congressman investigating claims that people were being held in the community against their will.

Schizophrenia and violence

The Jonestown massacre leads us to the other major reason for our fear of mental illness. In the minds of most people, mental illness, and in particular schizophrenia, is strongly associated with violence. This fear has always been with us. In another of his dialogues, Plato reports that

> When Socrates was told that there were many mentally disordered people in Athens he retorted 'how could we live in safety with so many crazy people? Should we not long ago have paid the penalty at their hands, and have been struck and beaten and endured every other form of ill usage which madmen are wont to inflict?'

The perception of madness today is little different. Here is the voice-over from the opening of the horror film *Schizo*

> Schizophrenia . . . a mental disorder, sometimes known as multiple or split-personality, characterized by loss of touch with the environment and alternation between violent and contrasting behavior patterns.

This perpetrates two of most widely held misperceptions of schizophrenia. First, that this is the same as multiple personality. Unfortunately, most people do not know that the term 'schizophrenia' was intended to capture the idea of a split between the components of one mind (knowledge, emotion, and will) rather than the idea of one mind splitting into several minds. Second, that an accurate picture of madness is contained in Robert Louis Stevenson's story in which the good Dr Jekyll turns into the evil and violent Mr Hyde. As we have seen, this is not the case.

This association with violence is typical in media representations of mental illness. A survey of American TV dramas in the 1980s found that 73% of the mentally disordered were displayed as violent. Reports in the tabloid press also reflect this attitude. During the last decade, violent events involving patients with schizophrenia have received maximum press coverage. Ben Silcock climbed into the lion enclosure at London Zoo and was severely mauled. Sharon Campbell killed her social worker when she was working late at night in the hospital. Christopher Clunis killed a man unknown to him who happened to be waiting for a train on the platform at Finsbury Park underground station.

As a result of these high-profile cases, the tabloid press seems to have belatedly discovered that when the large Victorian mental hospitals were closed down the patients who had lived there were moved into the community. A series of stories were published giving the impression that these patients were roaming the streets armed with knives and it was just a matter of time before they killed an innocent bystander. Typical headlines include: 'Knife Schizo'; 'Misfit with a Machete'; 'Psycho Killer'. As a result of this pressure, in 2000 the government proposed reforms to the Mental Health Act that would allow for the compulsory care and treatment of patients who were at 'high risk' of causing serious harm to others. As shown in Figure 21, the tabloids reacted with great enthusiasm.

There was one good consequence of this campaign about the treatment of people with schizophrenia. Attention was drawn to the fact that many patients were not receiving adequate care in the community. There is a desperate need for improvement in community care, and it may well be that, for many patients, short-term or long-term care in hospital may be more appropriate. However, this does not require that they should be 'caged' or locked up.

I'LL SWEEP PSYCHOS OFF THE STREETS

Dobson to cage 'timebomb' fiends

Dobson . . . aims to save lives

Stone . . two savage murders

By GEORGE PASCOE-WATSON
Deputy Political Editor

EXCLUSIVE

INCURABLE psychopaths like hammer killer Michael Stone will be locked up indefinitely under new laws announced today.

In a historic move, Health Secretary Frank Dobson will order secure hospital units to be built to cage fiends whose

personality disorders cannot be controlled by treatment.

In extreme cases, the key will be thrown away and the monster will die in the unit.

Hundreds of killers and perverts are in jail for murder or rape — but they are not medically ill and cannot be treated without consent.

Police and social workers consider them "timebombs" because they know they will strike again.

Under current laws, they can be released from jail when their sentence is over — allowing them to prey on the innocent again.

And they cannot be arrested until they commit a crime.

But Mr Dobson's £30-million reform package will mean they can effectively be jailed in the new units if doctors convince a court they are a serious risk.

Mr Dobson — who will also provide more beds for the mentally ill aims to stop a repeat of the case of madman Stone, 38. He was free to kill Kent mother Lin Russell, 45, and her daughter Megan, six, despite asking to go into hospital.

And as part of the bid to sweep psychos off the streets, the Care in the Community scheme will also be altered — so disturbed patients can be FORCED to take medicine if necessary.

FRAUD-BUSTERS TO HIT NHS

MINISTERS yesterday vowed to stamp out prescription fraud which costs Britain £150million a year.

Tens of thousands of operations are forgone each year because of the mas-

sive cost of NHS swindles.

One GP issued bogus prescriptions worth £700,000, while an optician claimed fees for dead patients.

New Health Minister Alan Milburn has recruited

regional fraud-busting teams to halve the problem within four years.

He said: "Those who exploit the system are cheating taxpayers and depriving patients of care."

---

21. Tabloid headline: 'I'll sweep them off the streets, Dobson to cage "timebomb" fiends.'

Care in crisis as mental patients are freed to kill

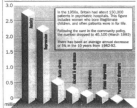

Mental illness in Britain

In the 1950s, Britain had about 150,000 patients in psychiatric hospitals. This figure includes women who bore illegitimate children, and often patients were in for life.

Following the care in the community policy, the number dropped to 45,100 (March 1992)

There has been an average annual decrease of 5% in the 10 years from 1982-92.

Ann: Survived sex and drug abuse

FOR 20 years, Margaret fought to save her mentally ill daughter, Ann, from sexual and drug abuse before into the community. She says:

She was a beautiful 24-year-old when she developed mental illness and was admitted to the Farringdon Wing of Luton Hospital.

She did not know my husband and I. She used to roam around in the same clothes week in, week out. No one cared for her and her condition deteriorated rapidly.

On at least six occasions, social workers set her up in dirty backstreet lodgings, sometimes without telling us. We went to visit and found her hair lice-ridden and clothes filthy. We were ashamed. She was not taking her medication and was being preyed upon by men. We tried everything to get the Social Services to take action, but nothing was done until three years ago, when we persuaded a doctor from Luton to recommend her to a rehabilitation unit.

They gave her care and made sure she took her medication, slowly bringing her back into reality. She is recovering and becoming the person we once knew.

LIEZE GETNING

Gareth died in confusion

GARETH was released from a psychiatric hospital under the Department of Health and Social Security's Care In The Community programme.

He was assessed by doctors and pronounced fit enough, under medication, to return to society.

He went to live with his mother Rosemary, in her sixties, but Gareth started acting strangely.

He became sinister, taking the kitchen knives and arranging them in neat lines on the table, touching them menacingly each day and moving them closer to his mother.

Rosemary discovered that Gareth, through lack of supervision, had stopped taking the medication which controlled his mood swings.

Her terror grew.

An emergency call to the hospital brought a refusal to take him back because he had chosen to be at home. Psychiatrists would not listen to Rosemary because she was not the patient. And the Social Services would take no action because Gareth hadn't done anything. But in more lucid moments, he was showing bouts of frustration, frequently becoming desperate at the thought of what he might do.

Despairingly, his mother put him on a bus back to the hospital. On the way, Gareth jumped off in a panic and disappeared.

The hospital was not interested — he was no longer a patient. The police didn't want to get involved. Social Services refused help, saying he was under hospital care.

His body was found floating in a river.

This tragic death became just another statistic. The catalogue of errors was forgotten.

Everyone who let him down gets off the hook and there is no inquiry to ensure it won't happen again.

Gareth suffered from schizophrenia, the most common mental illness, which fills more hospital beds than any other disease. One person in 100 throughout the world suffers from it at some time.

OF A COMMUNITY THAT IS FAILING TO COPE

FIRE: Ogilvie

RICHARD OGILVIE, a 29-year-old paranoid schizophrenic, was a potential killer from an early age, according to his mother.

He had been known to walk around the streets with a knife.

After seven years in care he was released. He set fire to the bed in a hostel where he was staying and was sent to hospital in the annexe of Wormwood Scrubs prison.

VIOLENT: Inweh

ERNI INWEH, a schizophrenic woman with a history of violence, stabbed to death a psychology graduate doing voluntary work in a charity hostel for the mentally ill. Violent patients would normally be refused a hostel place, but asked if Inweh had demonstrated life threatening behaviour, her social worker replied "No", believing that this meant suicidal tendencies. Inweh was sent to Broadmoor

GRADUATE: Gore

CHRISTOPHER GORE, a mathematics graduate, killed his father as he lay in bed of the family's home. Then he attacked his mother before repeatedly stabbing them and trying to set fire to the house. Psychiatrists said he had become mentally ill in childhood and developed schizophrenia. He was convicted of manslaughter and ordered to be detained indefinitely at Broadmoor high-security hospital.

---

22. Tabloid headline about violence and mental illness: 'Care in crisis as mental patients are freed to kill.' *Daily Express*, 22 September 1994.

What is the truth about schizophrenia and violence?

The justification for locking up people with mental illness is that this will reduce violence and save lives. But what is the association between schizophrenia and violence? This has been examined in a number of studies and the results are reasonably consistent. There is a small, but significant association between violence and schizophrenia. In any one year, about 8% of patients with this diagnosis and no other problems will commit an act of violence. This is lower than the association with other mental illnesses such as depression or personality disorder, but is higher than that found in people without mental illness, which stands at about 2%. There is a much higher association between violence and drug abuse (including alcohol), and for patients with schizophrenia who also have problems with drugs and alcohol the association can rise to 30%.

However, these figures must be put into the context of the causes of violence as a whole. If we ask what proportion of violent acts is perpetrated by patients with schizophrenia, then the answer is 3 or 4%. If we ask about the risk that a particular patient with schizophrenia will commit homicide, then the answer is less than 1 in 3,000, which is tiny. Assuming that about 4% of violent acts are committed by patients with schizophrenia, then, even if all these could be eliminated, that would still leave 96% of violent acts unaffected.

Managing risk

If we are to prevent violence by patients, we need to know why that violence happens and which patients are at risk for committing violence. A number of studies suggest that acts of violence typically occur during periods when patients are actively suffering from what are called 'threat' or 'control override' symptoms. In other words, the patients either believe that people are trying to harm them or experience their mind as being dominated by forces outside their control. One example would be the case of the painter Richard Dadd already mentioned in Chapter 3. Richard Dadd killed his father because he believed him not to be his father but an agent of the devil. On the other hand, many patients experience voices and commands telling them to commit violent acts. It is striking that the vast majority of them are able to resist these instructions.

Some acts of violence might be prevented if there was a greater understanding of the nature of the symptoms associated with schizophrenia. This applies particularly to paranoid delusions in which patients believe that people, often those in authority like the police and or the secret service, are trying to harm them. The problem is illustrated by a tragic case in the United States in which a man shot dead two policemen who broke into his house after complaints that he was playing loud music.

In his closing remarks, the defence attorney explained that FZ had a long-standing paranoid delusion that people – including the police – were out to get him. He called this a 'siege mentality'. Police were 'throwing gasoline on the fire' when they broke FZ's storm window and opened his door, the defence attorney said, causing FZ to respond with extreme anger borne of violent mood swings and paranoid schizophrenia. 'For FZ with his mental illness, this is his worst nightmare.' At one point in the defence attorney's statements, FZ blurted out a comment about police 'stalking and falsely arresting me. That's what I was up against.'

In order to prevent violence, we also need to be able to identify which patients are at risk, so that the limited available resources can be concentrated upon them. Patients at risk for committing violence can certainly be identified, but not on an individual basis. Patients are more likely to be violent if they have committed violence in the past, if they have stopped taking their medication, if their delusions encourage violence towards certain people, and if they have access to these people. By assessing risk in this way it is often possible to predict which patients will commit future episodes of violence.

About 17% of a group identified to be at high risk for violence are likely to commit violence in the future, whereas only about 3% of a low-risk group will do so.

Unfortunately, it is not at all clear that knowledge of these risk factors can help us to reduce violence. Relatively few patients with schizophrenia are at risk for committing violence. In these circumstances our predictions of who will be violent, although better than chance, are simply not good enough. A typical scenario might be as follows. In a sample of 500 patients, 8% (about 40) might be considered to be at risk for committing violence. This leaves 460 patients considered not to be at risk. Of the 40 patients at risk, 17% (about 7) will actually commit acts of violence. Of the 460 patients not at risk, 3% (about 14) will also commit acts of violence. In this example, the majority of the acts of violence have been committed by patients who were not identified as being at risk. This is a problem that arises in many circumstances, not just in relation to mental illness. Whether we are discussing violence and schizophrenia or train crashes, risks can never be reduced to zero. But on the other hand, how is it possible to have an 'acceptable' level of risk when that risk is of death?

The analysis we describe above has direct consequences for the day-to-day provision of psychiatric care. There is now a requirement that, whenever a mentally ill patient commits a homicide, there is a public enquiry. These enquiries typically find that the patient involved had received inadequate care from the community team – there was a lack of monitoring of the patient and his compliance with treatment, there was a lack of communication between different agencies, and so on.

The message is that community mental health teams should be identifying patients at risk for committing violence and concentrating their resources upon them. In an area of South London covered by two multi-disciplinary community teams, Shergill and Szmukler identified 90 patients (out of 318) who were at risk on the grounds that they had previously been violent towards another person. Weekly contacts with key workers for all these high-risk patients would have used up more than half of all the available resources. Yet this concentration of resources would be inappropriate for the 75 of the 90 who are probably not going to commit further acts of violence. At the same time, the remaining 228 patients who were not at risk would, of necessity, be seen much less frequently. But about 10 of these patients might also commit acts of violence. In the worst case, this could lead to another public enquiry and further criticism of the lack of care. This problem will not be solved by legislation. What is needed are greater resources for the appropriate management of patients and increased understanding of the nature of schizophrenia.

The mind and the brain

In this book we have emphasized the biological nature of schizophrenia. We have presented the evidence that this disorder stems from an abnormality in the brain that has a genetic basis. We have presented the evidence that the severity of the positive symptoms of the disorder, the hallucinations and delusions, can be increased and decreased by treatment with specific drugs. In order to explain these observations we have to accept that mental entities such as will and belief are the product of processes in the brain.

Many people find this idea very disturbing. At least since Descartes we have treated the physical and the mental as independent domains that involve entirely different kinds of process. This distinction has led to a number of false assumptions.

One assumption is that physical illnesses respond to physical treatments (like drugs) while mental illnesses respond to psychological treatments (like cognitive behaviour therapy). It follows that, if a major mental illness like schizophrenia has a physical basis, then there is not a place for psychological treatments. The false assumption here is that, while physical processes can cause changes in the mental domain, mental processes cannot cause changes in the physical domain. We see no logical reason why cause should not also flow from the mental to the physical and, furthermore, there is evidence for this direction of flow.

Patients with obsessive-compulsive disorder become obsessed with narrow themes, including thoughts of contamination by dirt or germs, worries that the doors are unlocked or the stove has been left on. These obsessions are associated with compulsions like hand washing or checking that can seriously interfere with daily life. In these patients, treatment with drugs *and* treatment with behaviour therapy can be effective. Using PET, Baxter and his colleagues showed that the physical treatment and the mental treatment produced the same changes in brain activity. This is a direct example of how a psychological treatment can affect brain function in the same way as a physical treatment, and shows that demonstrating causal links between brain and mind does not necessarily support reductionism. Reductionism, in this case, implies that understanding physical processes is sufficient to explain mental processes. The link can equally support expansionism, in which mental processes are sufficient to explain physical processes.

Responsibility

Another strong assumption is that we are responsible for the things that happen in our minds, but not for the things that happen in our brains. When we consciously and deliberately choose to perform one act rather than another, then we can be held accountable for that act. But our brains can cause us to do things for which we are not responsible.

Automatisms are common features of epilepsy. These are repetitive, meaningless movements that occur during a seizure. At the time the person is not aware of making the movements, and has no recollection of them after recovery from the seizure. These automatisms can sometimes take the form of quite complex actions and can be misunderstood by bystanders, for example, one sufferer started having a seizure while he was standing in a newsagents' shop. He began making automatic arm movements that swept everything from the counter on to the floor. He recovered from the seizure to find himself lying on the floor where the newsagent held him until the police arrived. He had no recollection of what had happened during the seizure.

In the case of epilepsy, we know that the automatic behaviour is caused by overactivity in an area of the brain that has been damaged. It is generally accepted, as happened in the case described above, that people with epilepsy should not be held responsible for the actions that they perform without awareness during seizures. We accept that the actions in these cases are caused by a damaged brain and are not the conscious and deliberate acts of a mind.

It is easy to accept that people should not be held responsible for an action if they were not aware of what they were doing at the time and there is a clear brain abnormality that caused the action. But the patient with schizophrenia is well aware of the acts he is performing and, although we believe they are influenced by brain abnormality, we cannot yet demonstrate precisely what this abnormality may be. Nevertheless, it has long been accepted that madmen should not be held responsible for their actions.

> If a madman or a natural fool or a lunatic in the time of his lunacy has no knowledge of good or evil and he does kill a man, this is not a felonious act.
>
> R v. William Lambarde (1581)

The madman has no knowledge of good or evil in relation to a particular act because of his delusions ('Immovable assumptions as to matters of realities', R. v. Hadfield, 1800). The point being made here is that, because of his delusion, the madman does not recognize that his act is morally wrong. He therefore has no criminal intent (mens rea). For example, Richard Dadd, the Victorian painter who killed his father, did not have the intent to kill his father. His intent was to kill the devil that he believed had taken on the form of his father.

The principle that delusions can eliminate criminal intent was enshrined in the McNaghten Rules of 1844. For a verdict of Not Guilty by Reason of Insanity:

> at the time of the act the party accused was labouring under such a defect of reason from disease of the mind as to not know the nature and quality of the act, or if he did know it, that he did not know he was doing what was wrong.

Of course, a person found not guilty by reason of insanity is still removed from society in order to prevent any further harm that might result from his continuing to act on the basis of delusions. However, he will be removed to a special hospital, such as Broadmoor, rather than a prison.

The idea that guilt depends upon criminal intent has the interesting consequence that the court has to make a decision about what was in the mind of the accused person. Most of the time our knowledge of what is in the minds of other people derives from what they tell us. We have already made the point that a psychiatrist can only know if a patient is experiencing delusions and hallucinations because the patient is prepared to talk about them. But in the context of a criminal prosecution, can we rely on someone to tell the truth about what is in his or her mind?

This problem was foremost in the trial of Peter Sutcliffe, known as the Yorkshire Ripper, who killed at least 13 women. Before the trial Sutcliffe was seen by four psychiatrists who all agreed that he was suffering from paranoid schizophrenia. Initially the Crown prosecution was willing to accept a plea of not guilty to murder but guilty of manslaughter on the grounds of diminished responsibility. However, the judge did not accept this and the case went to trial by jury.

Sutcliffe claimed that he had a divine mission to kill prostitutes and heard the voice of God telling him to kill. If the claim was true then, the judge directed, it was appropriate to find Sutcliffe not guilty of murder on the grounds of diminished responsibility. The key question for the jury to decide was whether this claim was true. The judge emphasized that the only evidence that Sutcliffe was deluded came from Sutcliffe himself.

> Mr Justice Boreham: ' . . . at the time of the killings, did he believe he was directed or instructed by God to kill prostitutes? Put in another way, did he, though deluded, believe that he was acting under a divine mission to kill prostitutes? [or] did he lie to the doctors in order to persuade them he was mad?'

The jury decided that Sutcliffe was lying. He was found guilty of murder and sent to prison for 30 years. After three years he was transferred to a special hospital.

The problem for the psychiatrists in this case was that their only evidence for the claim that Sutcliffe was acting from delusions came from his own report. But it is likely that within a few years studies of brain structure and function will provide us with objective evidence for the presence of delusions. At this point the defence in such cases will point to the brain abnormality as the proof of the presence of the abnormality of mind leading to diminished responsibility. This raises the question of where we draw the line.

Even if we are not deluded, conscious, deliberate actions don't occur all by themselves. There is a specific brain system that is associated with such acts. Furthermore, changes in brain activity can be detected before the commission of simple acts of this type. These changes occur even before the actor is aware of making the decision to act. If brain activity is the cause of decision-making, does this eliminate personal responsibility and free will? We do not believe so. But in that case we cannot make decisions about degree of personal responsibility simply in terms of brain function. Developments in neuroscience, especially as these apply to mental disorders like schizophrenia, are going to have ethical implications of which, as yet, we are only dimly aware.

Problems of responsibility also arise in relation to treatment. When should we honour the decision of patients to reject treatment? When is it appropriate to treat patients against their will? Having been presented with all available information about the advantages and disadvantages of treatment, a patient might make a deliberate and justified decision to refuse treatment. Patients with cancer and other life-threatening illnesses sometimes do this. It would be appropriate to honour such a decision, and if this is a persistently held view it is generally honoured. Such a decision is another example of a deliberately chosen act for which the individual can be held responsible. These are the sorts of decisions for which a 'sound mind' is required. There are obvious cases where, because of temporary or permanent damage to the brain, the mind is not considered sound. The patient might be unconscious or delirious. The patient might no longer be able to make an informed decision due to loss of intellect, as in dementia.

Patients with schizophrenia often refuse treatment and will present vociferous and justified reasons for doing so. In most of these cases, doctors will recommend that the patients' wishes should be disregarded. This is justified on the basis that the illness causes diminished responsibility for decisions about treatment, just as in the criminal cases we have just been considering. It is the very illness for which treatment is recommended that causes the patients' judgement to be impaired so that they do not appropriately understand the advice given to them about treatment. This is a very different situation from a patient with cancer who considers that the possible benefits of treatment in terms of extending his life are outweighed by the suffering likely to be caused by the treatment.

The delusions held by patients with schizophrenia diminish their ability to make rational decisions about treatment. Consider again the case of L. Percy King. He was firmly convinced that the voices he heard were real, not hallucinations. Therefore he was sane and did not need treatment. Another patient, J. Thomas, described how his 'voices' warned him against treatment – 'They are going to weaken and possibly kill you with their treatments'; 'They are blunting your mind'; 'Soon you will be a harmless cabbage'.

In these and similar cases, the delusions and hallucinations are directly affecting the patients' decisions about treatment. If we accept that delusions can reduce the patient's responsibility for his actions in criminal cases, should we not also accept that delusions could also reduce the patient's responsibility for his decisions about treatment?

In medical ethics the objection to treating people against their will is based on the principle of respect for autonomy. But people who are no longer fully responsible for their actions in consequence of their delusions have, by definition, lost their autonomy. To have autonomy we must be rational agents who are free to determine the course of our thoughts and actions, and a person with delusions is not wholly free to determine the course of his thoughts and actions. In this case, treatment, even if it is against the patient's expressed wishes, can be seen as an attempt to restore that patient's autonomy. After recovery, many patients, although not all, will accept that the treatment has helped them.

The importance of schizophrenia

There are many obvious reasons why the study of schizophrenia is important. Schizophrenia affects large numbers of people and causes great suffering. The cost to the state in terms of treatment and lost earnings is very high. The causes of schizophrenia remain unknown, and fully effective treatments remain to be developed. But the study of schizophrenia is also important because it confronts us with fundamental problems that are relevant to all of us, even if we never have contact with people who have schizophrenia. What is the nature of reality? How do we acquire knowledge and beliefs? To what extent are we responsible for our own actions? In this chapter we have shown how the study of schizophrenia raises all these questions, but we have not, of course, answered them. What the study of schizophrenia suggests is that these questions are closely linked with the problem of the relationship between the brain and the mind. The disorder that causes schizophrenia lies precisely in that region where brain and mind interact. It is not surprising that the basis of schizophrenia is proving so difficult to discover.

References

Chapter 1

Treatment of schizophrenia in the tabloid press: E. C. Johnstone,
C. P. L Freeman, and A. K. Zealley, *Companion to Psychiatry Studies*,
6th edn. (Churchill Livingstone, Edinburgh, 1998).

The incidence of schizophrenia throughout the world: A. Jablensky,
'Schizophrenia – Recent Epidemiologic Issues', *Epidemiological
Reviews* (1995), 17 (1): 10–20.

The cost of schizophrenia: L. M. Davies and M. F. Drummond,
'Economics and Schizophrenia – the Real Cost', *British Journal of
Psychiatry* (1994), 165: 18–21, suppl. 25.

'I am more and more losing contact': A. J. Lewis, 'The
psychopathology of insight', in *Inquiries in Psychiatry: Clinical and
Social Investigations* (Routledge and Kegan Paul, London, 1967),
pp. 16–29.

The writings of George Trosse and John Perceval: Dale Petersen (ed.),
A Mad People's History of Madness (University of Pittsburgh Press,
1982).

P. Pinel, Traité Médico-Philosophique sur l'Aliénation Mentale
(Brosson, Paris, 1809).

J. Haslam, *Observations on Madness and Melancholy*, 2nd edn. (John Callow, 1809).

B. A. Morel, *Traité des Maladies Mentales* (Masson, Paris, 1860).

Chapter 2
Development of the concept of schizophrenia: G. Berrios and R. Porter (eds.), *A History of Clinical Psychiatry* (Athlone Press, 1995).

E. Kraepelin, 'Dementia praecox and paraphrenia', tr. in *The Clinical Routes of the Schizophrenia Concept*, ed. J. Cutting and M. Sheperd (Cambridge University Press, 1987).

E. Bleuler, 'Dementia praecox or the group of schizophrenias', tr. in *The Clinical Routes of the Schizophrenia Concept*, ed. J. Cutting and M. Sheperd (Cambridge University Press, 1987).

Pseudo-neurotic schizophrenia: P. Hoch and P. Polatin, 'Pseudoneurotic forms of schizophrenia', *Psychiatric Quarterly* (1949) 23: 248–56.

US/UK diagnostic project: J. E. Cooper et al., 'Psychiatric diagnosis in New York and London', *Maudsley Monograph 20* (Oxford University Press, 1972).

DSM-IV: American Psychiatric Association, *Diagnostic and Statistical Manual of Mental Disorders*, 4th edn. (Washington DC, American Psychiatric Association, 1994).

Present State Examination: J. K. Wing, J. E. Cooper, and N. Sartorius, *Description and Classification of Psychiatric Symptoms* (Cambridge University Press, 1974).

Schneider's first rank symptoms: C. S. Mellors, 'First-rank symptoms of schizophrenia', *British Journal of Psychiatry* (1970), 117: 15–23.

Is there a form of schizophrenia with a good outcome?: E. C. Johnstone et al., 'The nature of "transient" and "partial" psychoses: findings from the Northwick Park "Functional" Psychosis Study', *Psychological Medicine* (1996), 26: 361–9.

The Northwick Park first episode study: J. F. MacMillan, T. J. Crow, A. L. Johnson, and E. C. Johnstone, 'Northwick Park study of first episodes of schizophrenia III. Short-term outcome in trial entrants and trial eligible patients', *British Journal of Psychiatry* (1986), 148: 128–33.

The outcome of schizophrenia: World Health Organization, *Schizophrenia: An International Follow-up Study* (John Wiley & Sons, New York, 1979).

Edinburgh high-risk study: E. C. Johnstone et al., 'Edinburgh high-risk study – findings after four years. Demographic, attainment and psychopathological issues', *Schizophrenia Research* (2000), 46: 1–15.

The genetic 'spectrum' of schizophrenia: K. S. Kendler et al., 'The structure of schizotypy – a pilot multitrait twin study', *Psychiatry Research* (1991) 36: 19–36.

Chapter 3

The central executive: A. Baddeley, *Working Memory* (Oxford University Press, 1986).

IQ in schizophrenia: C. D. Frith, J. Leary, C. Cahill, and E. C. Johnstone, 'Performance on psychological tests. Demographic and clinical correlates of the results of these tests', *British Journal of Psychiatry* (1991), suppl. 13: 26–9, 44–6.

IQ decline in schizophrenia: J. Rabinowitz et al., 'Cognitive and behavioural functioning in men with schizophrenia both before and shortly after first admission to hospital – cross-sectional analysis', *British Journal of Psychiatry* (2000), 177: 26–32.

IQ and institutionalization: E. C. Johnstone et al, 'The dementia of dementia praecox', *Acta Psychiatrica Scandinavica* (1978), 57: 305–24.

IQ and community care: C. Kelly et al., 'Nithsdale Schizophrenia Surveys 20 – cognitive function in a catchment-area-based population of patients with schizophrenia', *British Journal of Psychiatry* (2000), 177: 348–53.

IQ and drugs: S. Mohamed et al., 'Generalized cognitive deficits in schizophrenia – a study of first-episode patients', *Archives of General Psychiatry* (1999), 56(8): 749–54.

The core cognitive impairment in schizophrenia: B. Elvevag and T. E. Goldberg, 'Cognitive impairment in schizophrenia is the core of the disorder', *Critical Reviews in Neurobiology* (2000), 14(1): 1–21.

Motivation in schizophrenia: S. G. Hellman et al., 'Monetary reinforcement and Wisconsin Card Sorting performance in schizophrenia: why show me the money?', *Schizophrenia Research* (1998), 34(1–2): 67–75.

Single case approach: T. Shallice, P. W. Burgess, and C. D. Frith, 'Can the neuropsychological case-study approach be applied to schizophrenia?', *Psychological Medicine* (1991), 21: 661–73.

Classifying symptoms: T. J. Crow, 'Molecular pathology of schizophrenia: more than one disease process?', *British Medical Journal* (1980), 280(6207): 66–8.

Intellectual functioning and symptoms: E. C. Johnstone and C. D. Frith, 'Validation of three dimensions of schizophrenic symptoms in a large unselected sample of patients', *Psychological Medicine* (1996), 26(4): 669–79.

Genius and madness: N. C. Andreasen, 'Creativity and mental illness: prevalence rates in writers and their first-degree relatives', *The*

American Journal of Psychiatry (1987), 144(10): 1288–92; A. M. Ludwig, 'Creative achievement and psychopathology: comparison among professions', *American Journal of Psychotherapy* (1992), 46(3): 330–56.

Superior abilities in the relatives of patients with schizophrenia: J. L. Karlsson, 'Mental abilities of male relatives of psychotic patients', *Acta Psychiatrica Scandinavica* (2001), 104(6): 466–8.

Chapter 4

Amphetamine psychosis: P. H. Connell, *Amphetamine Psychosis* (Maudsley Monographs, 1958); S. Tatetsu, 'Metamphetamine psychosis', in *Current Concepts of Amphetamine Abuse*, ed. E. H. Elinwood (Rockville NIMH, 1972).

Experimental studies of amphetamine: J. D. Griffith, J. H. Cavanaugh, J. Held, et al., 'Experimental psychosis induced by the administration of d-amphetamine', in *Amphetamine and Related Compounds*, ed. E. Costa and S. Garattini (Raven Press, 1970), pp. 897–904; B. M. Angrist and S. Gershon, 'The phenomenology of experimentally induced amphetamine psychosis: Preliminary observations', *Biological Psychiatry* (1970), 2: 95–107.

Amphetamine and dopamine: L. Kokkinidis and H. Anisman, 'Amphetamine psychosis and schizophrenia – a dual model', *Neuroscience and Biobehavioral Reviews* (1981), 5 (4): 449–61.

Cannabis and schizophrenia: S. Andreasson, A. Engstrom, P. Allebeck, and U. Rydberg, 'Cannabis and schizophrenia – a longitudinal study of Swedish conscripts', *Lancet* (1987), 2 (8574): 1483–6; W. Hall and L. Degenhardt, 'Cannabis use and psychosis: a review of clinical and epidemiological evidence', *Australian and New Zealand Journal of Psychiatry* (2000), 34 (1): 26–34.

The cannabis receptor: M. Glass, 'The role of cannabinoids in neurodegenerative diseases', *Progress in Neuro-Psychopharmacology and Biological Psychiatry* (2001), 25 (4): 743–65.

PCP and schizophrenia: D. C. Javitt and S. R. Zukin, 'Recent advances in the phencyclidine model of schizophrenia', *American Journal of Psychiatry* (1991), 148 (10): 1301–8.

Discovery of antipsychotic drugs: J. Delay and P. Deniker, 'Le traitement des psychoses par une méthode neuroleptique dérivée de l'hibernothérapie', in *Congres de Médicins Aliénistes et Neurologistes de France*, ed. P. Cossa (Maisson Editeurs Libraires de l'Académie de Médicine, Paris, 1952), pp. 497–502.

Efficacy of antipsychotic drugs: J. M. Davis and D. L. Gerver, 'Neuroleptics – clinical use in psychiatry', in *Handbook of Psychopharmacology Vol 10. Neuroleptics and Schizophrenia*, ed. L. L. Iversen and S. D. Iversen (Plenum Press, 1978).

Dopamine and Parkinson's disease: O. Hornykiewicz, 'Dopamine in the basal ganglia. Its role and therapeutic implications (including the clinical use of L-DOPA)', *British Medical Bulletin* (1973), 29: 172–8.

The dopamine theory of schizophrenia: A. Carlsson and M. Lindquist, 'Effect of chlorpromazine and haloperidol of formation of 3-mcthoxytyramine and normetanephrine in mouse brain', *Acta Pharmacol. Toxicol.* (1963): 140–4.

Dopamine blockade and the efficacy of antipsychotic drugs: P. Seeman et al., 'Antipsychotic drug doses and neuroleptic/dopamine receptors', *Nature* (1976), 261: 717–9.

Atypical antipsychotics: J. Kane, G. Honigfeld, J. Singer, and H. Meltzer, 'Clozapine for the treatment-resistant schizophrenic. A double-blind comparison with chlorpromazine', *Archives of General Psychiatry* (1988), 45: 789–96.

A revised dopamine theory of schizophrenia: S. Kapur and
G. Remington, 'Dopamine D(2) receptors and their role in
atypical antipsychotic action: still necessary and may even be
sufficient', *Biological Psychiatry* (2001), 50: 873–83.

Imaging dopamine receptors: M. Laruelle, 'Imaging dopamine
transmission in schizophrenia. A review and meta-analysis', *Quarterly
Journal of Nuclear Medicine* (1998), 42: 211–21.

Chapter 5

Neuropathology of schizophrenia: Paul J. Harrison, 'The
neuropathology of schizophrenia: A critical review of the data and their
interpretation', *Brain* (1999), 122: 593–62.

Genetics of schizophrenia: I. I. Gottesman, *Schizophrenia Genesis: The
Origins of Madness* (W. H. Freeman & Co, 1991).

Adoption studies: S. S. Kety et al., 'Mental illness in the biological
and adoptive families of adopted individuals who have become
schizophrenic: a preliminary report based on psychiatric
interviews', *Proceedings of the Annual Meeting of the
American Psychopathology Association* (1975), 63:
147–65.

Genetic linkage studies: K. S. Kendler, 'The feasibility of linkage
studies in schizophrenia', in *Biological Perspectives of Schizophrenia*,
ed. H. Helmchan and F. A. Henn (Wylie, 1987).

Susceptibility genes in schizophrenia: C. R. Cloninger, 'The discovery of
susceptibility genes for mental disorders', *Proceedings of the National
Academy of Sciences, USA* (2002), 99: 13365–7.

Velo-cardio facial syndrome: K. C. Murphy and M. J. Owen, 'Velo-cardio
facial syndrome. A model for understanding the genetics and
pathogenesis of schizophrenia', *British Journal of Psychiatry* (2001),
179: 397–402.

Enlarged ventricles in schizophrenia: S. Lewis, 'Structural brain imaging in biological psychiatry', *British Medical Bulletin* (1996), 52: 465–73; S. M. Lawrie and S. S. Abukmeil, 'Brain abnormality in schizophrenia. A systematic and quantitative review of volumetric magnetic resonance imaging studies', *British Journal of Psychiatry* (1998), 172: 110–20.

Gliosis in schizophrenia: G. W. Roberts et al., 'Is there gliosis in schizophrenia? Investigation of the temporal lobe', *Biological Psychiatry* (1987), 22: 1459–68.

Brain changes prior to onset of schizophrenia: S. M. Lawrie et al., 'Brain structure, genetic liability, and psychotic symptoms in subjects at high risk of developing schizophrenia', *Biological Psychiatry* (2001), 15: 811–23.

Functional brain imaging in schizophrenia: S. M. Lawrie, 'Neuropathology and brain imaging in schizophrenia', in *Schizophrenia: Concepts and Clinical Management*, ed. E. C. Johnstone, M. Humphries, F. Lang, S. M. Lawrie, and R. Sandler (Cambridge University Press, 1999), pp. 70–128.

Brain connectivity: K. J. Friston, 'Dysfunctional connectivity in schizophrenia', *World Psychiatry* (2002), 1: 66–71.

Chapter 6

Psychodynamic theories of schizophrenia: P. J. McKenna, *Schizophrenia and Related Syndromes* (Psychology Press, 1997).

Social stress as a cause of schizophrenia: G. W. Brown and J. L. Birley, 'Crises and life changes and the onset of schizophrenia', *Journal of Health and Social Behaviour* (1968), 9: 203–14; M. Malzacher, J. Merz, and D. Ebnother, 'Marked life events prior to an acute schizophrenic episode. Comparison of a sample of first admissions with a normal sample', tr. by authors, *Archiv für Psychiatrie und Nervenkrankheiten* (1981), 230: 227–42.

Family relationships as a cause of schizophrenia: L. Wynne and M. Singer, 'Thought disorder and family relations of schizophrenics. I. A research strategy. II. A classification of forms of thinking', *Archives of General Psychiatry* (1963), 9: 191–206; S. Hirsch and J. P. Leff, 'Abnormalities in the parents of schizophrenics' (*Maudsley Monograph No. 22*, Oxford University Press, 1975).

Institutionalization and schizophrenia: D. G. Cunningham Owens and E. C. Johnstone, 'The disabilities of chronic schizophrenia – their nature and the factors contributing to their development', *British Journal of Psychiatry* (1980), 136: 384–95; D. A. Curson, C. Pantellis, J. Ward, and T. R. E. Barnes, 'Institutionalisatism and schizophrenia, 30 years on', *British Journal of Psychiatry* (1992), 160: 230–41.

Gender differences in schizophrenia: H. Hafner et al., 'Generating and testing a causal explanation of the gender difference in age at first onset of schizophrenia', *Psychological Medicine* (1993), 23: 925–40.

Season of birth and schizophrenia: T. N. Bradbury and G. A. Miller, 'Season of birth in schizophrenia: a review of evidence, methodology, and etiology', *Psychological Bulletin* (1985), 98: 569–94.

Maternal flu and schizophrenia: E. O'Callaghan et al., 'Schizophrenia after prenatal exposure to 1957 A2 influenza epidemic', *Lancet* (1991), 337: 1248–50; R. E. Kendell and I. W. Kemp, 'Maternal influenza in the etiology of schizophrenia', *Archives of General Psychiatry* (1989), 46: 878–82.

Famine and schizophrenia: E. S. Susser and S. P. Lin, Schizophrenia after prenatal exposure to the Dutch Hunger Winter of 1944–1945', *Archives of General Psychiatry* (1992), 49: 983–8.

Birth complications and schizophrenia: J. R. Geddes and S. M. Lawrie, 'Obstetric complications and schizophrenia: a meta-analysis', *British Journal of Psychiatry* (1995), 167: 786–93.

Chapter 7

The abyss of understanding: K. Jaspers, *General Psychopathology* (Manchester University Press, 1962).

Hallucinations as subvocal speech: L. N. Gould, 'Auditory hallucinations and subvocal speech', *Journal of Nervous and Mental Disease* (1949), 109: 418–27; P. Green and M. Preston, 'Reinforcement of vocal correlates of auditory hallucinations by auditory feedback: a case study', *British Journal of Psychiatry* (1981), 139: 204–8.

Inner speech: A. D. Baddeley and G. J. Hitch, *Working Memory. The Psychology of Learning and Motivation: Advances in Research and Theory* (G. H. Bower Academic Press, 1974), pp. 47–90.

Articulation as a treatment for auditory hallucinations: H. E. Nelson, S. Thrasher, and T. R. Barnes, 'Practical ways to alleviate auditory hallucinations', *British Medical Journal* (1991), 302: 327.

Hallucinations and inner speech: C. L. Evans, P. K. McGuire, and A. S. David, 'Is auditory imagery defective in patients with auditory hallucinations?', *Psychological Medicine* (2000), 30(1): 137–48.

Brain activity and inner speech: P. K. McGuire et al., 'Functional anatomy of inner speech and auditory verbal imagery', *Psychological Medicine* (1996), 26: 29–38; D. A. Silbersweig et al., 'A functional neuroanatomy of hallucinations in schizophrenia', *Nature* (1995), 378: 176–9; S. S. Shergill et al., 'Mapping auditory hallucinations in schizophrenia using functional magnetic resonance imaging', *Archives of General Psychiatry* (2000), 57(11): 1033–8.

The concept of corollary discharge: H. von Helmholtz, *Handbuch der Physiologischen Optik* (Leipzig, Voss, 1866).

Self-monitoring and schizophrenia: I. Feinberg, 'Efference copy and corollary discharge: implications for thinking and its disorders', *Schizophrenia Bulletin* (1978), 4: 636–40; C. D. Frith, 'The positive and negative symptoms of schizophrenia reflect impairments in the perception and initiation of action', *Psychological Medicine* (1987), 17(3): 631–48; R. P. Bentall, G. A. Baker, and S. Havers, 'Reality monitoring and psychotic hallucinations', *British Journal of Clinical Psychology* (1991), 30: 213–22.

Self-monitoring and motor control: P. Haggard, C. Newman, and E. Magno, 'On the perceived time of voluntary actions', *British Journal of Psychology* (1999), 90: 291–303; C. D. Frith and D. J. Done, 'Experiences of alien control in schizophrenia reflect a disorder in the central monitoring of action', *Psychological Medicine* (1989), 19(2): 359–63.

Imagining movements and schizophrenia: P. Maruff, P. Wilson, and J. Currie, 'Abnormalities of motor imagery associated with somatic passivity phenomena in schizophrenia', *Schizophrenia Research* (in press).

Tickling and schizophrenia: S.-J. Blakemore et al., 'The perception of self-produced sensory stimuli in patients with auditory hallucinations and passivity experiences: evidence for a breakdown in self-monitoring', *Psychological Medicine* (2000), 30: 1131–9.

Brain activity and self-generated sensations: S. A. Spence et al., 'A PET study of voluntary movement in schizophrenic patients experiencing passivity phenomena (delusions of alien control)', *Brain* (1997), 120: 1997–2011; J. M. Ford et al., 'Cortical responsiveness during talking and listening in schizophrenia: An event-related brain potential study', *Biological Psychiatry* (2001), 50(7): 540–9.

The disconnection hypothesis: S. M. Lawrie et al., 'Reduced frontotemporal functional connectivity in schizophrenia associated with auditory hallucinations', *Biological Psychiatry* (2002), 51(12): 1008–11; J. M. Ford et al., 'Reduced communication between frontal and temporal lobes during talking in schizophrenia', *Biological Psychiatry* (2002), 51(6): 485–92; K. J. Friston, 'Dysfunctional connectivity in schizophrenia', *World Psychiatry* (2002), 1: 66–71.

The anarchic hand: C. Marchetti and S. Della Salla, 'Disentangling the alien and anarchic hand', *Cognitive Neuropsychiatry* (1998), 3: 191–208.

Other minds: R. Corcoran, G. Mercer, and C. D. Frith, 'Schizophrenia, symptomatology and social inference: Investigating "theory of mind" in people with schizophrenia', *Schizophrenia Research* (1995), 17: 5–13.

Capgras syndrome: G. Blount, 'Dangerousness of patients with Capgras syndrome', *Nebraska Medical Journal* (1986), 71: 207; H. D. Ellis and A. W. Young, 'Accounting for delusional misidentifications', *British Journal of Psychiatry* (1990), 157: 239–48.

Weird experiences are not enough: C. Cahill, D. Silbersweig, and C. D. Frith, 'Psychotic experiences induced in deluded patients using distorted auditory feedback', *Cognitive Neuropsychiatry* (1996), 1: 201–11.

Efficacy of drug treatment: J. M. Davis and D. L. Gerver, 'Neuroleptics – clinical use in psychiatry', in *Handbook of Psychopharmacology. Neuroleptics and Schizophrenia*, ed. L. L. Iversen and S. D. Iversen (Plenum Press, 1978).

Efficacy of psychological therapies: S. Pilling et al., 'Psychological treatments in schizophrenia: I. Meta-analysis of family intervention and cognitive behaviour therapy', *Psychological Medicine* (2002), 32(5): 763–82; S. Pilling et al., 'Psychological treatments in schizophrenia: II. Meta-analyses of randomized controlled trials of social skills training and cognitive remediation', *Psychological Medicine* (2002), 32(5): 783–91.

Cognitive therapy for hallucinations: P. D. J. Chadwick and M. J. Birchwood, 'Challenging the omnipotence of voices: a cognitive approach to auditory hallucinations', *British Journal of Psychiatry* (1994), 164: 190–201.

Chapter 8

L. Percy King, 'Criminal complaints with probable causes (a true account)', in *The Inner World of Mental Illness*, ed. Bert Kaplan (Harper & Row, 1964).

The immunity principle: S. Gallagher, 'Self-reference and schizophrenia: a cognitive model of immunity to error through misidentification', in *Exploring the Self*, ed. D. Zahavi (John Benjamins, 2000).

Hallucinations caused by direct brain stimulation: H. W. Lee et al., 'Mapping of functional organization in human visual cortex – Electrical cortical stimulation', *Neurology* (2000), 54: 849–54.

Rational justifications for delusions: A. Baddeley et al., 'Schizophrenic delusions and the construction of autobiographical memory', in *Remembering Our Past: Studies in Autobiographical Memory*, ed. D. C. Rubin (Cambridge University Press, 1996), pp. 384–428.

Folie à deux: R. Mentjox, C. A. van Houten, and C. G. Kooiman, 'Induced psychotic disorder: clinical aspects, theoretical considerations, and some guidelines for treatment', *Comprehensive Psychiatry* (1993), 34: 120–6.

Violence and mental illness on television: G. Gerbner, L. Gross, M. Morgan, and N. Signorielli, 'Health and medicine on television', *The New England Journal of Medicine* (1981), 305: 901–4.

Violence and schizophrenia: E. Walsh, A. Buchanan, and T. Fahy, 'Violence and schizophrenia: examining the evidence', *British Journal of Psychiatry* (2002), 180: 490–5.

Predicting violence in schizophrenia: S. S. Shergill and G. Szmukler, 'How predictable is violence and suicide in community psychiatry practice?', *Journal of Mental Health* (1998), 7: 383–401.

Inquiries into failures of community care: Louis Blom-Cooper, 'The falling shadow: one patient's mental health care 1978–1993', report of the Committee of Inquiry into the events leading up to and surrounding the fatal incident at the Edith Morgan Centre, Torbay, on 1 September 1993 (Duckworth, 1995).

Drug treatment and psychological treatment have the same effect on the brain: L. R. Baxter et al., 'Caudate glucose metabolic-rate changes with both drug and behavior-therapy for obsessive-compulsive disorder', *Archives of General Psychiatry* (1992), 49: 681–9.

Diminished responsibility: The insanity defence allows for the acquittal of an accused who is felt not to be responsible for his actions. However, it sets a high threshold. Before the abolition of the death penalty in 1965, in murder cases where mental disorder was felt to be a major mitigating factor, but where an insanity defence could not be achieved, the individual would hang. Dissatisfaction with this situation led to the importation of 'diminished responsibility' from Scotland under the Homicide Act 1957. Diminished responsibility sets a lower threshold than insanity, but leads to a conviction for manslaughter rather than an acquittal. For diminished responsibility there must be 'such abnormality of mind . . . as substantially impaired his mental responsibility'. The 'abnormality of mind' necessary can be interpreted widely, and certainly covers all aspects of a psychotic illness that may lead to homicide. Since the replacement of execution by a mandatory life sentence for murder, diminished responsibility remains the most popular psychiatric defence in these types of cases.

Brain activity during acts of will: C. D. Frith et al., 'Willed action and the prefrontal cortex in man', *Proceedings of the Royal Society of London* (1991), B: 241–6; B. Libet et al., 'Time of conscious intention to act in relation to onset of cerebral activity (readiness-potential). The unconscious initiation of a freely voluntary act', *Brain* (1983), 106: 623–42.

Further reading

Chapter 1

The experience of madness: Bert Kaplan (ed.), *The Inner World of Mental Illness* (Harper & Row, 1964); Dale Petersen (ed.), *A Mad People's History of Madness* (University of Pittsburgh Press, 1982); Roy Porter (ed.), *Faber Book of Madness* (Faber and Faber, 1993).

The history of madness: Roy Porter, *Madness: A Brief History* (Oxford University Press, 2002); Roy Porter, *Mind-forg'd Manacles: A History of Madness in England: 1669–1810* (Athlone Press, 1987).

Chapter 2

More detailed accounts of the development of the concept of schizophrenia: P. J. McKenna, *Schizophrenia and Related Syndromes* (Psychology Press, 1997); Eve C. Johnstone et al., *Schizophrenia: Concepts and Clinical Management* (Cambridge University Press, 1999).

Chapter 3

The central executive and its slave systems: A. Baddeley, *Human Memory: Theory and Practice* (Oxford University Press, 1990).

The concept of intelligence and IQ: Robert J. Sternberg, *Handbook of Intelligence* (Cambridge University Press, 2000).

The use of neuropsychological tests to localize brain function: Ros A. McCarthy and Elizabeth K. Warrington, *Cognitive Neuropsychology: A Clinical Introduction* (Academic Press, 1990).

Intellectual function and neuropsychology of schizophrenia: Chris Frith, *The Cognitive Neuropsychology of Schizophrenia* (Psychology Press, 1992).

The relationship between genius and madness: Kay Jamison, *Touched with Fire: Manic-Depressive Illness and The Artistic Temperament* (Free Press, 1996).

The best novel about schizophrenia: Einar Már Gudmundsson, *Angels of the Universe*, tr. Bernard Scudder (Mare's Nest, 1995).

Chapter 4

Hallucinations associated with alcohol abuse: I. Solares, *Delirium Tremens: Stories of Suffering and Transcendence*, tr. T. G. Compton (Halzelden, Center City, 1979).

A romantic account of the effects of hallucinogenic drugs: A. Huxley, *The Doors of Perception and Heaven and Hell* (Penguin Books, 1959).

An excellent introduction to the mechanisms of drug action: Stephen M. Stahl and Nancy Munter, *Essential Psychopharmacology of Antipsychotics and Mood Stabilizers* (Cambridge University Press, 2002).

Chapter 5

Especially good on the evidence for the genetic basis of schizophrenia: I. I. Gottesman, *Schizophrenia Genesis: The Origins of Madness* (W. H. Freeman & Co, 1991).

Provides a brief history of the search for the biological basis of schizophrenia as well as an account of the author's early work on this topic: E. C. Johnstone, *Searching for the Causes of Schizophrenia* (Oxford University Press, 1994).

Chapter 6

Vivid accounts of how family and social relationships might cause schizophrenia: R. D. Laing, *The Divided Self: A Study of Sanity and Madness* (Tavistock Publications, 1960); R. D. Laing and A. Esterson, *Sanity, Madness, and the Family* (Viking Press, 1964, reissued 1990).

Presentation of the arguments that justified the closure of the large asylums in the 1980s: J. K. Wing and G. W. Brown, *Institutionalism and Schizophrenia* (Cambridge University Press, 1970).

Chapter 7

The argument that schizophrenia does not really exist is presented most forcefully in Mary Boyle, *Schizophrenia, A Scientific Delusion?* (Routledge, 1990), but we are not convinced.

For an account of the role of subvocal speech and self-monitoring in hallucinations, see Chris Frith, *The Cognitive Neuropsychology of Schizophrenia* (Psychology Press, 1992).

A description of the 'articulatory loop' can be found in A. Baddeley, *Your Memory: A User's Guide* (Prion Books, 1996).

A number of interesting neurological disorders, including the anarchic hand and Capgras syndrome, are described in *Method in Madness*, edited by Peter Halligan and John Marshall (Psychology Press, 1996). This book also contains some useful chapters about schizophrenia.

For an account of cognitive therapy, see Judith Beck, *Cognitive Therapy* (Guilford Press, 1995). An excellent guide to the use of cognitive therapy with schizophrenia is provided by Hazel Nelson, *Cognitive Behavioural Therapy with Schizophrenia: A Practice Manual* (Nelson Thornes, 1997).

Chapter 8

The trial of Peter Sutcliffe: A comprehensive account of this trial can be found on *http://www.execulink.com/~kbrannen/trial01.htm*

Medical ethics: Allen E. Buchanan and Dan W. Brock, *Deciding for Others: The Ethics of Surrogate Decision Making* (Cambridge University Press, 1989). A general theory for treatment decisions for incompetent patients, especially minors, the elderly, and psychiatric patients.

For a popular account of recent research relating the brain and the mind, see Rita Carter, *Mapping the Mind* (Weidenfeld & Nicolson, 1998).

Index

D

Visit the
VERY SHORT
INTRODUCTIONS
Web site

www.oup.co.uk/vsi

➤ **Information** about all published titles

➤ News of **forthcoming books**

➤ **Extracts** from the books, including titles
  not yet published

➤ **Reviews** and views

➤ **Links** to other **web sites** and main
  OUP web page

➤ Information about **VSIs in translation**

➤ **Contact** the editors

➤ **Order** other **VSIs** on-line